Beekeeping for Beginners

How to Raise Your First Bee Colonies to Make Your Hive Thrive!

Written By Rohn Garden

TABLE OF CONTENTS

CHAPTER 1

All about Honey Bees

Perhaps the ideal approaches to turn into a decent bee-keeper is to all the more likely comprehend the animals you're managing. Bees have become increasingly more essential to people in ongoing decades, and because their endurance is continually in danger, find out about the indispensable job they play in our lives will help beekeepers wherever guarantee they keep on prospering.

In this part, you'll find out about the physiological changes that happen in honeybees dependent on breed, sex, and position. You'll additionally find out about the significance of bees for human endurance just as how the state capacities overall. It's astounding how 40,000 bees can cooperate on shared objectives all with the wellbeing of the whole province on a fundamental level.

WHY WE NEED HONEYBEES

Despite their name, honeybees accomplish more than making delightful honey. They're likewise liable for 33% of the world's nourishment flexibly just like the endurance of plants and trees. What's more, they may very well be the best superorganism good examples for Earth's animals, including people.

Honeybees fertilize more than $15 billion worth of harvests in the United States every year. Indeed, beekeepers lease more than 2.5 million settlements every year for the fertilization of around 90 distinctive US crops, particularly almonds, apples, horse feed seed, and vegetables. These yields develop on about 3.5 million sections of land, and they mean 33% of our everyday diet and honeybees ensure those nourishments stay in plentiful gracefully. Bees usually are dynamic regardless of what season it is, which means people can have confidence realizing we'll have nourishment all year.

Bees fertilize blossoms more than some other creepy-crawly and more than any other plant. Shockingly, bee fertilization needs nourishment to endure and that all starts with fertilization. As a working drone moves from bloom to blossom, drinking nectar, she catches up on against anthers loaded with dust, which run to the hairs covering her body. As she flies along, she starts brushing the dirt with her legs and moving it to the dust bins (CORBICULA) on her rear legs. During that procedure, she accidentally drops a portion of the dust back onto different blossoms, causing fertilization.

BEES HAVE SUPERPOWERS

The province works all together to manage hive temperatures and move air around and through the hive to cool it, heat it, or acquire more oxygen. They some of the time search up to 6 miles in a solitary excursion. They gather water what's more, control dampness; they construct the cells inside their home for nourishment stockpiling and raising their kin bees; they care for their sovereign and her brood; what's more, they settle on aggregate choices about what dust or nectar sources to search or where to make their next home on the off chance that they move. They additionally give an entire state of mind control through the sharing of hormonal emissions and sovereign substances from bee to bee.

THE HONEYBEE SUPERORGANISM

A province of bees is ordinarily alluded to as a superorganism because they're eusocial animals that have a profoundly specific division of work, and individual bees can't endure alone for broadened timeframes. Honeybees are social creepy crawlies and capacity as an aggregate gathering living and cooperating in a state. Albeit every bee experiences its stages and periods of life and has singular assignments to finish, the province prosperity, in general, decides most bee conduct.

About 80% of plants utilize biotic fertilization, which means the plants need assistance from other living animals, (for example, creatures or creepy crawlies) to move the dust. Be that as it may, different plants, for example, grasses, conifers, and some deciduous trees, use abiotic fertilization usually wind and now and then water.

Regular Species of Honeybees

Not all bees are the equivalent, and few out of every odd bee produces honey. Indeed, they're called honeybees for an explanation, and it's everything about that sweet nectar and the fertilization procedure. There are numerous subspecies of honeybees, and every ha its unique attributes and practices.

THE WESTERN HONEYBEE

Even though the honeybee variety contains a few animal types, this book centres around the most widely recognized honeybee on the planet: the Western honeybee. At first, you would have discovered this species just in Africa, Europe, or Asia. In any case, when individuals began to import bees to other geographic regions, numerous subspecies or geographic races started to create. The Western honeybee, however, has remained the most widely recognized bee for beekeepers due to its accommodating nature, its honey-creating ability, and it's advantageous boss interaction. As beekeeping turned out to be increasingly mainstream, beekeepers started to search out bees dependent on their most attractive qualities: shading, size, reasonableness to a region, a measure of honey gathered, personality, swarm affinity, utilization of propolis (tar bees gather), and protective practices. This prompted tests in rearing for particular characteristics. Such half breeds as Buckfast, Starline, Midnight, Cordovan, Russian, and even the Africanized bees have all been created from rearing and interbreeding for attractive attributes. Albeit a portion of the half and halves, for example, Starline and Midnight, are not, at this point accessible, others are as yet being tried and created in severe reproducing programs all through the United States.

Italian and Carniolan bees are as yet the most widely recognized honeybees bought by US beekeepers, however, with new research concentrating on bee ailments and parasites, science is nearly rearing more grounded bees with better bug resilience and opposition. This should prompt guaranteeing honeybees proceed to flourish and offer this world their fertilization enchantment.

THE HONEYBEE HIVE

The honeybee hive is a mind-boggling system of frameworks and signs; however, the reason for existing is straightforward: make a situation where the province can endure and flourish. Honeybee endurance necessitates that they find and keep a reasonable area to manufacture their home of wax looks over for raising a brood and for putting away nourishment. They lean toward that home area to be inside a cavity, for example, in a tree, in the ground, or a human-made structure. A settlement will, in general, have two primary requirements for endurance:

1) Find a suitable hive area where bees can accumulate and, all the more significantly, store nourishment to endure all year, particularly when bee scavenge is rare, for example, during a brutal winter or during severe flooding or dry spells all limits that can undermine settlement endurance.

2)   Propagate hereditary qualities through automaton creation and conceptive amassing otherwise called throwing swarms.

In the wild, bees incline toward home destinations need to be cosy so they can secure and safeguard their settlement, yet they likewise need space to develop and for honey stockpiling. They as often as possible pick locales that were recently involved by different honeybees, particularly on the off chance that they have old brushes that are prepared to utilize. Bees can practically cause their home anyplace were they to feel like they'll have enough space to store nourishment and remain warm yet less space that they won't have the option to safeguard their home appropriately.

When a province picks an area, the bees go option to work, fixing breaks and covering the internal dividers with propolis, which weatherproofs the hive as well as include antimicrobial and anti-fungal properties that help keep a hive stable. The bees likewise cooperate in the colony to keep up legitimate temperatures for brood raising, which can include warming or cooling the hive contingent upon occasional temperatures.

When they've picked their new home, the honeybees start assembling their brushes by joining four to eight brushes to the tops or sides of the house. Brushes are developed corresponding to each other and have around 1 centimetre between everyone, which is called bee space. This permits the bees space to stroll around and watch the home without finding each other.

Making honeycomb is a high vitality utilization task, so honeybees attempt to be effective in their endeavours. Deliver 2.2 pounds (1kg) of honeycomb, so their first year in another area is frequently the most troublesome because they're typically beginning without any preparation. Not exclusively will they need loads of honey stores to fabricate their house, yet they'll likewise need to start putting away enough honey to endure their first winter.

Movement in the beehive never stops. Bees are consistently busy working—building, cleaning, evaluating, securing, taking care of the sovereign and her brood, and looking for more nourishment sources. It's no big surprise they're the hotspot for the phrase "occupied as a bee."

Phases of Honeybee Development

In the same way as other creepy crawlies, honeybees experience improvement stages from birth to grown-up. Their life expectancies rely upon the capacities they perform, yet it's the sovereign and the sorts of eggs she lays that choose every bee's job—and its destiny.

EGG

When working drones survey a state's needs, they'll assemble wax cells in differing sizes to address those issues. The sovereign can then rapidly quantify a cell's format to recognize what sort of egg to lay: A prepared egg brings about a female bee, and an unfertilized egg brings about a male bee. This egg stage goes on for around three days.

Female bees are diploid, which means they have two arrangements of chromosomes one each from their mom and father. Male bees are haploid, which means they have one lot of chromosomes from only their mom. This hereditary cosmetics probably won't mean a lot to the sovereign. However, it turns into a factor for the eggs she lays.

Hatchling

Following three days, the egg hatches into a hatchling that is likewise called a first instar. The modest hatchling will lay in the base of the cell in a C-formed position. The hatchling needs bountiful measures of nourishment and starts developing right around multiple times its size each day. For the first day, all the new hatchlings are taken care of a rich eating regimen of illustrious jam. If the hatchling is to turn into a sovereign, she stays on a tight eating routine of renowned jam. However, the labourers and automatons change to brood nourishment a blend of dust and honey. Taking care of hatchlings is consistent work, and bees will visit every hatchling roughly multiple times during the initial 8 to 10 days of hatchlings life.

Life Cycle of the Honeybee

A run of the mill province has somewhere in the range of 20,000 to 60,000 bees, with a more significant part of them being females called working drones. Contingent upon the season, what's more, the state's prosperity, a province additionally has around 300 male bees called rambles. Be that as it may, a settlement can just have one sovereign—and she's the mother of the considerable number of bees in that province. Every one of these bees has a new job, and outstanding burden inside the hive and everyone has an alternate life cycle.

PUPA

Around eight days after their introduction to the world, labourer hatchlings are topped closed in their cells. On a ninth day, the hatchlings turn a silk cover produced using a glandular emission in their mind. On the tenth day, the hatchlings lay back and position their heads toward the highest point of the cell opening to finish their prepupal stage. On the eleventh day, a fifth shed happens, leaving the pupae white. The bees bit by bit builds up their shading during the following week when they'll experience their 6th and last hut. This is the point at which the bees change from pupae to imago (the final grown-up stage) and berate their method for their cells.

Each of the three positions/phases of bees—labourers, automatons, and sovereigns—start with a similar 3-day egg stage. They begin to vary with the sovereign having the briefest larval and pupal stages and the automaton having the longest stage. The honeybee life stages table is a critical indicative device for beekeepers to utilize when assessing hives for good sovereigns with great laying designs. All the variables that go into the raising of the egg, including diet, preparation, and cell size, will have an immediate outcome on what sort of grown-up rises out of the cell, its life expectancy, and its bigger job inside the hive.

The Queen Bee

Bee endurance relies upon a stable and glad sovereign. Even though the sovereign heads the settlement and has labourers and automatons to do her offering, she despite everything procures her keep by laying eggs day and night. In any case, she's something other than a mothering sovereign.

TURNING INTO A QUEEN

Any treated honeybee egg can turn into a working drone or a sovereign bee. This is called being totipotent, which means a solitary cell can gap to make all the phones inside a creature. At the point when working drones pick another sovereign, they search for a young hatchling and start taking care of it an eating regimen wealthy in an illustrious jam as opposed to the regular brood nourishment (a blend of honey, dust, and bee catalysts). This more burdensome eating regimen permits her to build up a more extended stomach area and more ovarioles (cylinders to the ovaries) than a working drone, and she's currently en route to turning into a sovereign.

A few attendants may cut a sovereign's wing to keep her from leaving the hive. Be that as it may if her wing is cut and the province chooses to crowd, she won't have the option to take off and may tumble to the ground when she attempts to leave. On the off chance that the settlement makes another little girl the sovereign, at that point, the new girl will execute the sovereign.

SOVEREIGN CUPS AND CELLS

Sovereign cups and cells can be anyplace in the hive. However, they're as a rule on brood brush. Sovereign cups are the beginning of a sovereign cell; however, without illustrious jam, eggs, or hatchlings in them. Numerous states have at least one sovereign cups on a couple of brushes as a kind of protection approach on the off chance that they have the motivation to make a sovereign. A sovereign cell is a prolonged cup that has been cleaned furthermore, sparkled, has regal jam covering the base, and has a hatchling in it that is being taken care of illustrious jam. A sovereign can lay up to twice her body weight in eggs each day, and she'll keep delivering eggs every day for a fantastic remainder, which can last somewhere in the range of 3 and 4 years. Throughout the spring, the sovereign now and again lays up to 2,000 eggs every day, rapidly pressing cells with little mouths to take care of.

The sovereign is anything but difficult to spot since she waddles over the brush with apparent reason, scanning for recently arranged and void cells in which to store eggs. She can have an assortment of hues just as groups on her midriff, yet she's frequently a strong shading without stripes. Contingent upon where you buy your sovereign from, you can request that the raiser mark her back with a shaded spot that relates to her introduction to the world year and solicitation them to slice one wing to keep her from taking off in a multitude.

For the sovereign to remain the main egg layer in the hive, she should discharge pheromone signs to the working drones. One of the significant pheromones is QUEEN MANDIBULAR pheromone (QMP), which the sovereign produces in the mandibular organ in her mind. QMP represses ovary improvement in the labourers and ends potential conceptive sovereign raising in the hive. It likewise instigates specialist entourage conduct and postpones searching conduct. Inside a couple of days to seven days after her introduction to the world, a recently incubated virgin sovereign leaves home on mating trips to ramble assembly regions, where she flies around and holds on to be trapped in mid-air and mated by rambles. She regularly takes a few distinctive mating trips before coming back to her home, where she'll spend a mind-blowing remainder laying eggs.

During these flights, she mates with numerous automatons, looking to gather enough spermatozoa (which treats the ovum) in her spermatheca (where sperm is put away) to keep going for her lifetime. The distinctive spermatozoa combine, and a few assortments are discharged as the sovereign releases her eggs to prepare future working drones. The subsequent working drones are groupings of relatives, each with the fluctuating qualities and attributes of their particular dad rambles. This decent automaton variety takes into account higher province endurance since certain automatons may have better-scrounging qualities and others better malady opposition.

THE DRONE BEE

Automaton bees the main guys in a state don't gather dust or nectar, and because they don't have stingers, they can't help safeguard the hive. Ramble bees have one singular assignment throughout everyday life: mating with a virgin sovereign to engender their hereditary qualities.

At the point when a settlement is progressing admirably, becoming more prominent, and has bunches of honey put away, your bees may start to go into conceptive multitude mode. At the point when this occurs, the working drones begin building bigger cells as a rule around the brush edges or in the unfilled spaces above or underneath an edge. The bigger cells are a sign to the sovereign to lay unfertilized eggs, which will end up being her children: the automatons. A settlement will ordinarily have only two or three hundred automaton bees since rambles are more prominent and they expend a more significant amount of the hive assets. Automatons are haploid, which means they as it were. This automaton is being taken care of by working drones. They additionally have bigger flight muscles and wing ranges for getting the sovereigns for mating. During cold winters, working drones will expel rambles from the settlement so they won't need to take care of all winter.

HOW DRONES MATE WITH QUEENS

To mate with a virgin sovereign, an automaton everts his endophallus inside a sovereign, which hinders him, and his penis bursts with a perceptible fly as he discharges semen into the sovereign's oviduct. The penis remains inside the flying sovereign, and the automaton tumbles to the ground, biting the dust presently. The following automaton to get the sovereign will expel the penis and rehash the procedure, permitting the sovereign to start to fill her oviduct with enough hereditarily differing spermatozoa to last her lifetime. Instead, they mate in ramble assembly regions that are 30 to 120 feet noticeable all around. These equivalent zones are utilized quite a long time after a year, even though it's obscure how new automatons find these territories without different automatons to control them. Automatons are once in a while nearer than 300 feet to an apiary and are regularly a lot more distant away. The automatons in an assembly zone can emerge out of upwards of 200 different provinces, and up to 25,000 individual automatons can make up one automaton gathering territory, along these lines expanding decent hereditary variety and diminishing the potential for inbreeding much further.

TO WHAT EXTENT DRONES LIVE

Automatons can meander from hive to hive and spend their evenings taking 30-moment to 1-hour trips to different automaton assembly territories to sit tight for virgin sovereigns. Under one automaton in 1,000 is effective in his mating mission; however, it isn't for the absence of endeavouring—there are only significantly a more significant number of automatons than sovereigns. These fruitless automatons will typically satisfy a half year. Effective automatons—as amusing as that sounds—bite the dust not long after mating what's more, in this manner have a lot shorter life expectancies.

The Worker Bee

Much like their name recommends, working drones play out all the everyday obligations that keep the hive running effectively. They're continually assessing the hive, searching for undertakings to finish and progressing in the direction of shared objectives with their hive sisters. In any case, don't excuse them as irrelevant in the settlement positions. They're the core of the state, and without them, sovereigns and automatons could never endure.

TURNING INTO A WORKER

A working drone takes around 21 days from egg to bring forth as a grown-up bee. All working drones are female and originated from prepared eggs. They get a large portion of their hereditary cosmetics from the sovereign bee and half from their automaton father. Since the sovereign mates with numerous automatons and stirs up all the sperm in her spermatheca, working drones in the province are always a blend of full and stepsisters. This decent variety makes a group of labourers with a more extensive assortment of hereditary qualities. Some will be better wax manufacturers, or dust foragers, or honey creators each contributing its solidarity to build settlement endurance.

Working drones have bunch occupations to perform, and they start directly after bring forth. Their first occupation is to clean out their introduction to the world cell and set it up for reuse. House bees spend nearly the initial three weeks of life working inside the hive, helping feed the new hatchlings, topping cells, taking care of their sovereign mother, delivering wax for brush building, maturing honey, cleaning, cooling, guarding, thus substantially more. As more bees incubate and can assume control over house occupations, labourers start to take direct flights. These are short round trips up what's more, around and afterwards withdraw to the hive. They're mapping their environmental factors and remembering everything close to their hive entrance so they can discover it again when they begin scavenging for nourishment.

Scavenging is critical for bee endurance. Forager bees search out nourishment for the hive, and they'll spend their whole lives as tracker gatherers. They'll scout inside a 2-to 3-mile span from the hive, looking for and gathering dust, nectar, water, and propolis for their states. At the point when assets are low in an inquiry territory, forager bees have been known to fly up to 6 miles looking for dust or nectar for settlement endurance.

THE BEEKEEPER'S NOTEBOOK

Since a bee's healthy wing flight life is around 500 miles, keeping your bees in zones where nourishment and water sources are close by can enable your bees to live and work longer. At the point when temperatures chill off and light hours abbreviate, the bees won't fly as frequently and can live any longer as long as a half year.

Deciding a working drone's life expectancy is, to some degree, complex. Yet, it relies upon average temperatures, removes the bees must fly for their assets, generally speaking, settlement well-being, karma in keeping away from predators, and that's only the tip of the iceberg. During times when nectar stream is plentiful, and the bees are speeding out and once again from dawn to nightfall, they may live for 2 to 3 weeks. The steady flying starts to shred their wings, and in the end, they're not, at this point ready to fly back to their hive and will bite the dust without their state.

At the point when you see a whirlwind of bees flying around your hives, you may think your bees are disordered, however together, they're a finely tuned machine, and the bee rank framework the sovereign, labourers, and automatons signifies every bee's particular capacities. This implies bees comprehend what they should regularly achieve to permit the hive to work productively.

HOW BEES COMMUNICATE

Since bees are a superorganism, they rely upon one another for endurance; openness is vital for ideal execution. Bees consistently screen a hive's status and transfer messages from bee to bee to expand their general profitability and to guarantee their future. Most correspondence happens using pheromones they discharge, go around the settlement, and distinguish with their intense feeling of smell utilizing their radio wires to smell each other as they stroll around the hive searching for work to do or to caution each other to potential dangers. They additionally go pheromones through taking care of practices a procedure is known as trophallaxis.

WHERE'S KING BEE?

There is no ruler bee in the hive. Initially, the sovereign bee was known as the ruler bee on account of its bigger size and evident significance in the province. Afterwards, analysts acknowledged she was female and the egg layer of the settlement. Sovereigns don't do much inside the hive except lay eggs, yet it's the most basic job a bee can play. Her egg-laying capacities decide the achievement and fate of not just the present bees in the hive; however, all the future ones as well.

Working drones are the ones who rule the hive. They settle on a few critical choices, including accessible hive space, accessible search nourishments, climate conditions, the wellbeing status of the hive, and even what sort of eggs the sovereign needs to lay. Automatons don't have stingers and don't gather nourishment for the hive. They have only one primary occupation: to mate with virgin sovereigns from different hives. Automatons can live from about a month and a half to a half year, yet once they mate with the sovereign, they bite the dust not long after. Much like people, bees speak with one another in different manners. Bees share data with different bees through physical and compound signs: development, vibration, contact, taste, and smell–all intended to advise different bees where to discover nourishment, regardless of whether they're at serious risk, and substantially more.

BEE SENSES

Honeybees see their general surroundings through different tangible upgrades, and they have an uncanny capacity to impart mind-boggling subtleties to their settlement to inform different bees regarding nourishment, dangers, and different circumstances. They're ready to outline their environmental factors with their inner GPS, and they utilize that data to convey the areas and kinds of nourishment sources they've found. Bees are delicate to scents and tastes, which assist them with finding nectar and dust sources as they rummage. They can see all the hues in the range except the shading red, which looks dark to bees. Honeybees can likewise observe the bright range, which helps them in discovering nourishment. They can even tell whether a bloom has just been as of late visited by another bee and along these lines keep away from it.

WHAT BEES EAT

32

The nature of nourishment your honeybees can find, devour, and store enormously impacts numerous parts of province life. What bees eat can decide their general wellbeing as well as the quality of their invulnerable frameworks, their development and advancement, and even their life span. It may appear as though bees produce honey for others' utilization, be that as it may, bees rely upon honey and different nourishments they reap and make for their own dietary needs. On the off chance that they can't get to dust, nectar, or water, they can't take care of their posterity—or themselves.

HONEY

Bees convert gathered nectar into honey their primary starch source to take care of developing hatchlings, even though the hatchlings picked to become future sovereigns are taken care of regal jam. Honey is likewise eaten by all bees for vitality and is a primary nourishment hotspot for bees during colder months. People likewise love honey, yet try to leave bounty for your bees and their nourishment needs.

BEE BREAD

Bees will turn dust alongside honey, nectar, and bee salivation into this matured nourishment that offers bees the protein they need. Bees mature dust to broaden its life expectancy since dust doesn't keep going long if not appropriately put away after being expelled from plants. This moreover enables the bees to have decent nourishment flexibly during colder months or when they're not able to collect dust or nectar for their eating regimen. All creating hatchlings are taken care of regal jam. Following three days, however, the working drones pick explicit hatchlings to become future sovereigns, and those hatchlings keep on being taken care of regal jam, with the other hatchlings being taken care of bee bread.

DUST

Dust is the protein source in the bee bread took care of to creating hatchlings, and it's likewise devoured by youthful medical attendant bees to finish their physical development. Dust is fundamental for sound glandular advancement in these young grown-up bees, whose organs, for example, the hypopharyngeal and mandibular organs, will before long produce imperial jam. On the off chance that the labourers can assemble a decent assortment of dust, that will likewise give all the minerals, nutrients, and amino acids expected to keep the settlement stable and sound.

NECTAR

Nectar gives bees the sugars or vitality required for flying and working. They blend it in with dust for bee bread to take care of their young, and they store it in the edges as topped honey for winter. They have to expend honey as they structure a defensive bunch around the sovereign and youthful brood in colder months while they cooperate to keep up a consistent temperature in the focal point of the brood home.

WATER

Water is additionally a key component of honeybee nourishment; they can't live for more than a couple of days without it. They need it for absorption to get the supplements they eat into their bodies, and they need it to expel squander from their bodies. Water is likewise used to condense granulated or thick honey and sugar, so it tends to be eaten, and water helps calm and humidify the hive during the hotter climate. Water ought to be given near the bee yard. Also, water can even be put in feeders on the hive during times of unusually blistering climate.

CHAPTER 2

Getting Started with Beekeeping

Beekeeping has developed from a crude side interest to artistic expression. Hundreds if not thousands of mechanical advances have happened over the most recent two centuries that have carried us into the cutting-edge time of beekeeping.

Over the most recent couple of years, there's been a resurgence of enthusiasm for specialist beekeeping individuals who need to keep a couple of settlements of their own for somewhat honey or perhaps just to assist the bees. In this section, you'll become familiar with the absolute most significant disclosures in beekeeping history and go through the sorts of hives accessible. You'll additionally find out about the devices and gear you'll require to begin, how to set up your beard, and how to get your first province of bees.

The Evolution of Beekeeping

While beekeeping appears to be a cutting-edge side interest, bees have been kept, and honey has been delighted in for a great many years. Our predecessors didn't have any of the innovative advances we have now for beekeeping. However, they did rapidly figure out how best to keep bees. Records from this timespan recommend that people ate honey and wax this far back ever. An apiary with round and empty hives dating from this time was found in Israel. Hives produced using earthenware dating from this century have been found in Greece. Rock artistic creations in

Spain from around this year show somebody moving up to an original hive to take honey. This ransacking approach proceeds right up 'til the present time in particular societies and with different bee species. Egyptians are demonstrated by smoking hives and gathering honey. During the 1500s through the 1800s, individuals utilized gums (tree trunks), skeps (woven bushels), and ceramics for hives. People pushed bees to the crowd to make much more hives apparently to create a higher amount of that heavenly honey.

In the nineteenth century, Europeans were, to some degree, partitioned in their beekeeping styles for the most part in light of the accessible materials for building hives. In the south, they utilized horizontal hives; in the north, they utilized upstanding log hives; and in the northwest, where trees were less bottomless, they utilized straw skeps. Present-day bee box structures have kept on bringing space into more thought. Two bees strolling consecutive on confronting brushes based on outlines have around 1 centimetre of room between them merely enough space for the bees not to have to occupy that space with wax.

BEE PROLIFERATION

Present-day beekeepers owe because of prior American nonconformists who helped beekeeping grab hold and extend in a nation doing likewise after the American Revolution. These imaginative men and their undertakings have suffered and keep on staying famous all through the side interest. In 1851, having a sharp comprehension of how bees use bee space, Langstroth expounded on his improved top-passage beehive structure. He found that if the dispersing over the edges is more than 1 centimetre, the bees will occupy the space under the top with a brush. On the off chance that space is littler than that, the bees will append propolis (bee stick) wherever to seal it shut.

By the following year, Langstroth had protected his structure for a versatile edge hive: a crate with ten edges and perfect space around the edges. His plan got typical all through the United States, Canada, and Europe. Despite specific adjustments to the structure throughout the years, this hive type keeps on bearing Langstroth's name.

Langstroth's hives implied higher honey yields and more benefit giving beekeeping its required toehold to turn into an increasingly business adventure. From the mid-1800s to the mid-1900s, beekeeping developments overflowed the market. One such development came to the kindness of Moses Quinby. In 1873, Quinby made a smoker with cries, permitting beekeepers to all the more effectively oversee and keep bees. Even though producers tinkered with the first structure from changing the handle to help forestall consume to adding airspace to the smoker to assist it with remaining lit longer—beekeepers despite everything use smokers, what's more, have Quinby to thank for the under-lying invention. First, human-made beehives were primarily containers flipped around. These hives–called skeps–had been the standard for around 2,000 years before Langstroth's structure.

41

PIONEERS OF BEEKEEPING

Even though Quinby sought to make beekeeping and honey creation a profitable endeavour, westbound extension and railroad transportation gave John S. Harbison an early beekeeper in California—the chance to send rail shipments around the United States conveying vast amounts of boxed brush honey. When trucks got typical, and beekeepers had more command over planning and item conveyance, beekeepers, made sense of they could move their bees north to make increasingly honey furthermore, south again to overwinter. It wasn't some time before ranchers began to see the estimation of bees for crop fertilization and would pay beekeepers to put the bees close to their yields, including one more route for beekeepers to bring in cash.

With industrialized cultivating came a developing interest for an ever-increasing number of bees, which implied the requirement for a superior arrangement of mass-delivering sovereigns. Gilbert M. Doolittle utilized the best of every realized strategy to make a framework for mass-delivering sovereigns. He empowered enormous scope sovereign creation, which started for the most part in the northern states yet, in the long run, moved south, where they had the benefit of a prior spring start. Delivery bees around the nation before long turned into the standard, and the bee bundle industry took off. Bundled bees, in the long run, turned out to be famous to the point that Sears and Roebuck sold bee bundles in their shopping lists.

Alongside beginning the magazine Gleanings in Bee CULTURE (today referred to just as Bee CULTURE), Amos Root established fabricate and sell beehives and beekeeper hardware. A portion of his magazine perusers would keep in touch with him around one

Of their creations, and he'd purchase the rights to it, make a couple of enhancements to the structure, and afterwards mass-produce and sell it. His organization, despite everything, exists today run by Root's extraordinary incredible grandson also, keeps on distributing Bee CULTURE magazine. The games groups at Medina High School in Medina, Ohio, utilize the epithet Battling Bees as a tribute to Root.

WHY BECOME A BEEKEEPER?

There are a considerable number of reasons concerning why individuals come to beekeeping as a side interest. Some desire the honey and the magnificent results of the hive, while others consider beekeeping to be an increasingly worldwide activity to spare bees and our planet.

You don't have to go Sparing BEES (AND THE WORLD) like all bugs; bees are under consistent danger from sickness, bugs, and natural and synthetic elements. Honeybees fertilize 90% of US crops, which people rely upon for their endurance. If we lose all the honeybees, our reality may likewise be at risk. In any case, we can help change that by getting progressively dynamic in helping bees flourish, attempting to support change in how and where harmful synthetics are utilized, and in any event, engaging your bees by giving them the required devices and situations wherein they can thrive and succeed.

POLLINATING YOUR GARDEN

45

Natural product trees developing on your property or maybe in a neighbouring yard, facilitating a beehive in your yard is gainful for the bees, and your nursery produces. You may even observe an expansion in the amount and nature of your vegetables the first year you begin keeping bees. You may likewise find that your bees will instinctually help blooming plants seed and develop in infertile regions and afterwards those regions may keep on prospering as long as your bees can appropriately tend and build up those plants.

REMOVING HONEY

Having your settlement is the ideal approach to guarantee you have delectable crude honey in its most original state. Honey takes its flavour profile from the plant's bees take nectar from. You can even plant explicit blossoms to carry their substances to your honey. You may even locate that honey in the spring doesn't taste equivalent to honey in harvest time.

You can likewise reap and extricate wax, dust, and nectar; you can assist bees with getting progressively invulnerable to illnesses when they're better shielded from dangers, and you can even help other people find how stunning beekeeping is only it in beekeeping. Bees clubs exist in each state and all through the world, and most have instructive open doors for new beekeepers. Bee clubs will frequently impart beekeeping assets to club individuals, for example, having a club extractor for credit or offering beekeeping books or assets that individuals can get to. I enthusiastically suggest joining a bee club and finding a guide to work with—both with your bees and with their bees to gain from somebody with more experience than you have.

URBAN BEEKEEPING

Beekeeping has encountered a flood in notoriety, and that flood remembers an extended enthusiasm for beekeeping in urban settings. In any case, urban beekeeping can regularly mean a higher number of limitations than rustic beekeeping, so realizing the guidelines will expand your potential for progress. Be a Good Neighbor

1) Let your prompt neighbours think about your arrangements they'll comprehend what's happening originating from your terrace.

2) Install a 6-foot security fence or support around your hives to constrain bee traffic to fly over neighbours' yards.

3) Minimize your bees' experiences with your neighbours by pointing hive doorways from zones frequented by human traffic and setting your hives far away from pet regions.

PICK THE RIGHT LOCATION

1)   It's ideal for putting hives on private property and away from high-thickness open spaces. If you don't possess the property, get authorization.

2)   With restricted space accessible at most urban areas, a few people need to have hives in different spots, including downtown housetops. Yet, before you investigate that situation, consider your security when wearing a suit with reduced permeability and when you may be occupied by bees. Perhaps you can convey light or void hardware up a stepping stool, yet shouldn't something be said about when you may need to convey an overwhelming hive loaded with bees and honey? Think about any and every single imaginable circumstance before you find a hive in a less open area.

3)   Make sure to have satisfactory close by water sources and plants for scavenging to keep your bees from neighbours' yards.

Know Your Local Laws

1)   Check with district and city specialists to realize what you may or may not be able to in an urban setting.

2)   Seek out a nearby affiliation or an accomplished neighbourhood beekeeper for data on what you're legitimately permitted to do in your city condition.

3)   Find out if your locale has any disturbance laws that may keep you from beekeeping in specific spots or circum-

stances.

Use Your Local Resources

Associate with a nearby beekeeping gathering. These similar individuals are an extraordinary asset for help moving a hive or then again in finding an elective area. Get ready for Potential Problems

1) While swarms are only occasionally protective, they can appear to be alarming to neighbours. Effectively oversee for swarm anticipation, and keep an extra hive close by forgetting a multitude if the need emerges.

2) Open taking care of syrup or honey can cause battling and cautious practices. It's smarter to take care of your bees while they're in their hives.

3) Robber screens can confine guarded conduct, yet have a reinforcement plan on the off chance that you have to move a hive. This may involve parting a hive or putting a hive higher off the ground.

Watered urban finishing can furnish your bees with nourishment sources on the off chance that they're starving throughout a mid-year shortage in an urban setting.

Rustic Beekeeping

Rustic cultivating has become well known once more, and that implies an ever-increasing number of individuals depend on bees for fertilization in these settings. Country scenes are perfect for starting beekeepers since you've likely previously arranged for giving bees what they require for their endurance.

1) You may have more opportunity to do certain things since

you live outside city limits, state and area laws you should comply.

2)   Consult with other country beekeepers about neighbourhood guidelines just as what number of hives they're ready to oversee while likewise running a ranch or doing their work in different manners.

Make the Right Environment

1)   Bees need a wide range of scavenging regions, so ensure that on the off chance that you have crops that you have an assortment of them instead of a couple.

2)   Having a bloom nursery will give your bees different chances to gather dust and nectar.

3)   Have something developing all year to guarantee your bees have nourishment to endure the winter, even though you can gather and store their dust to take care of them later.

4)   Don't disconnect your hives.

You ought to have the option to see every one of your hives from a window in your home. This will make your hives less welcoming to criminals who try to take honey or whole hives to coordinate their environmental factors to make them less noticeable to potential hoodlums. On the off chance that your hives aren't unmistakable as hives, they'll be even less welcoming to those explicitly searching for hives.

1)   Register your hives with a nearby position so you'll be advised when splashing has been planned which happens in territories with enormous scope rural cultivating. You would then be able to make strides to forestall damage to your bees. You can likewise ensure you place your hives

where they'll be less affected by crop tidying.

2)   Keep records of how the climate in your general vicinity is and what sort of predators exist just as what you did in those circumstances. So you can guarantee you're ready to determine any issues or get ready for any potential difficulty.

Beekeeping on a Careful spending plan

Before you decide to put resources into costly beekeeping hardware, there are some economic approaches to make natively constructed beekeeping things. Along these lines, you're not contributing more than you have to until you choose whether beekeeping is directly for you.

A few beekeepers can oversee bees on a careful spending plan, cobbling together hives from scrap wood and getting swarms, rather than buying the costliest gathered hardware, purchasing sovereigns with specific hereditary qualities, and in any event, employing hive-side counselling. Parity knowing where you can ration and where you can't be vital to fruitful beekeeping.

You can set aside some cash by building your gear. You can make simple tops and bottoms for Langstroth hives, what's more, even the containers and edges don't should be exact. Similarly, top-bar hives were intended to be worked by hand. Unassembled financial plan grade Langstroth boxes and top-bar units regularly sell for less from beekeeping flexibly organizations than the wood to make them would cost from a home improvement store. A readiness to invest a little energy utilizing paste, nails and paint can set aside your cash better utilized for other beekeeping needs.

Develop and require extra space for honey stores. If the territory has a wealth of honey, you can concentrate and return a super a similar season, sparing you the expense of the case and outlines and the bees' interest in drawing out the new brush. Abstain from disregarding your hives, and try to fix them at the main indications of difficulty. You leave hives to bear the components if wax moths assume control over your edges, or on the off chance that you generally handle hardware, you'll cause more costs by supplanting hives and gear than if you appropriately care for your speculations even economic ones.

While you can make your hives and use family things for hardware and your bee suit, you shouldn't hold back on the most significant part to beekeeping: purchasing bees. Buying better bee stock (or purchasing substitution bees) is a superior utilization of your cash than purchasing first-class hives or extra hardware. You ought to go through more cash each year on purchasing bees than everything else related to beekeeping. You won't require hives or gear on the off chance that you have second rate bees who all end up dead before a year. Putting resources into top-notch bees and sovereigns from trustworthy providers will deliver snappy profits when you're ready to benefit from their boss honey and wax. Request required hardware for almost any undertaking in late harvest time or late-fall since significant beekeeping flexibly organizations ordinarily have gear put in a raincheck for a little while in the spring when bees are their busiest.

THE BEEKEEPER'S TOOLSHED

While the instruments a beekeeper may require vary from individual to individual, some fundamental devices are necessary to claim. Start with these essential devices, and in time, you can grow your assortment to incorporate different less essential gear. One extraordinary approach to assist you with besting deal with your bees is to utilize a smoker. A smoker is an essential device for any starting beekeeper. It produces smokes that enables quiet bees and covers to caution pheromones that are discharged when a hive is upset.

1)   Heavy sheet metal for the body

2)   Durable inside and outside parts

3)   Effective plan, including an adequate roar

4)   Lid with a pivoted pin (instead of a creased metal piece) and a bolted wire circle handle

5)   Sizable internal firebox and a defensive watchman outwardly

Bee Brush

If your smoker goes out before you've shut a hive or on the off chance that you have to rapidly move bees off the beaten path to close a hive without crushing them, a bee brush is a valuable device, you'll discover different utilizations for it, including forgetting about ants or creepy crawlies your hives, even though it's particularly helpful for dismissing bees an edge when you're ransacking honey for extraction. Bees don't care for the bee brush, so pick one with delicate, standard fibres.

Individual experience will rapidly show you exactly how significant a smoker is. That one time you figure you won't need a smoker since you're going to open the hive for just a couple of moments or because you're in a rush is the point at which you'll get familiar with a difficult exercise one that stings in a more significant number of ways than one about how flighty bees are now and then.

Hive Tool

At the point when bees start to seal the hive with propolis the bee stick that likewise forestalls illness and contamination inside the hive, you'll need the hive device to pry among boxes and under edges that are covered with propolis.

Additional Tools

While the hive smoker, hive device, and bee brush should help you in any circumstance, some different apparatuses may prove to be useful:

1) Frame grasp: Used to snatch an edge in a top-bar hive and pull it from the hive for assessment

2) Hive bearer: Placed over the highest point of a hive stack to empower two individuals to lift a full arrangement of boxes

3) QUEEN cut: Allows you to catch and hold a sovereign—pick a reasonable plastic model to all the more effectively observe the sovereign

4)   QUEEN EXCLUDER: Keeps the sovereign from laying eggs where bees are making honey and are utilized during honey stream close to your hives. A hive device called a J-snare can likewise assist you with lifting outlines from a Langstroth hive.

Hive device

Frame spacer: Puts space among edges and comes in additional convenient on the off chance that you have one less edge in a hive and makes further wax cells, which bees will load up with a more significant amount of their heavenly honey

THE BEEKEEPER'S CLOSET

Picking fitting individual security apparatus will make beekeeping increasingly charming. When you can believe that you're appropriately shielded from potential stings, you can concentrate on keeping up your hives and thinking about your bees.

1) Shroud

2) Gloves

3) Individual Protective Gear

It's imperative to have a sense of security when you're in your beeyard. Standard assurance gear ensures your head, your body, and your hands, yet you can likewise purchase a suit that will secure your legs. Or on the other hand, you can purchase a coat and shroud or only a cover all alone. Attempt to discover a suit that furnishes you with viable ventilation and will persevere through substantial use. Albeit one-piece and two-piece suits exist, you may think that it's more straightforward to put on and remove a two-piece suit—and two-piece suits are progressively agreeable if you have to twist around for specific errands. Purchase a suit that is one size bigger than you'd ordinarily purchase to give you more opportunity for development. Ventilated suits help forestall stings yet keep you more relaxed in hotter climate. Even though it very well may be simpler to do some beekeeping errands without gloves, starting beekeepers should turn out to be increasingly agreeable around their bees and find out about their bees' practices before abandoning gloves. At times, being stung a couple of times will assist you with adapting to the torment faster.

Calfskin, material, and elastic. Test a couple out for adaptability and ability. You need your gloves to accomplish something beyond ensure your hands. A few people like to wear a couple of sets of nitrile gloves, which take into account high manual smoothness furthermore, are generally sting-verification. Be that as it may, they can make your hands hot and sweat-soaked, what's more, they're anything but difficult to tear.

Many cover styles exist, however, the most widely recognized are a collapsing shroud or a head protector and cloak (likewise called a SQUARE shroud), around cover, and Alexander cover, and a fencing or hooded shroud. A few covers have a worked in the cap. However, others can be pulled over the top of a cap. Round cover permits you to find in a 360° circle. However, it may be hard to see the ground before you. Many full suits accompany a hooded shroud. However, they work best with a baseball hat on to keep the face cloak from falling back onto your face while you're working.

One preferred position of a cover over a full bee suit with an incorporated shroud significantly more rapidly. What's more, that can prove to be useful on the off chance that you've been working for some time in a warm atmosphere and need to remove your cloak rapidly. To guarantee your shroud is a solid match, give it a shot in the splendid sun and in conceal and with your glasses on the off chance that you wear them.

THE LANGSTROTH HIVE

Albeit many hive types exist, the Langstroth hive configuration remains the standard for beekeepers. Langstroth outlines keep bees from interfacing brushes to different casings or hive dividers and along these lines making the edges more straightforward for you to oversee.

Picking a Box Size

Choosing an 8-or 10-outline width is a significant initial phase in choosing your Langstroth hives. Commonly, the two sizes cost about a similar sum. However, 8-outline hives proceed to pick up in prevalence since they don't weigh such a lot as 10-outline hives. Regardless of which size you pick, if every one of your hives is a similar width, at that point, you won't have any issues with contrary segments.

Picking a Hive Depth

Hive encloses come four profundities: profound, medium, shallow, and brush honey. Profound (95/8 inches) and medium (65/8 inches) boxes are the most widely recognized because they offer a lot of room for the bees. Profound boxes are commonly utilized for brood chambers are still in some cases called brood boxes. Medium boxes are frequently set on top (prevalent) for honey creation and are alluded to as SUPERS. You can likewise utilize shallow boxes (53/4 inches) or brush honey (45/8 inches) boxes. Whatever you use, bees couldn't care less and will utilize any size box for their brood or for putting away honey as they see fit.

THE BEEKEEPER'S PICKING BOTTOM BOARDS

Scratchpad:

Producers differ in their width of 8-outline encloses and how they isolate the bee space between the top and base in their cases. Staying with boxes from a solitary producer will guarantee the best fit (and give you the most straightforward time pulling them separated).

While arranging your hives, consider how overwhelming boxes maybe when loaded with honey. A 10-outline profound box brimming with honey gauges as much as 90 pounds, and an 8-outline medium box loaded with honey gauges around 45 pounds. They are utilizing every one of the 8-outline mediums guarantees that all parts are tradable what's more, that you don't need to lift a lot at any one time. Base sheets have indeed been loud, however, screened base sheets have developed as a component of an incorporated nuisance the board (IPM) technique and to build ventilation in the hive. The individuals who utilize screened base sheets that incorporate gadgets for checking bugs or catching hive beetles think of them as significant. Screened base sheets cost more and are more delicate than strong base sheets. Most large apiaries that utilization strong base sheets accept that the bees can control ventilation fittingly without the extra opening of a screened baseboard, and they use to bug the board systems that make a screened base pointless.

Transient spread or an extending spread. Enormous scope beekeepers utilize transitory top spreads since they permit them to put hives near one another on beds, empowering them to move those hives starting with one dust area then onto the next. Transitory spreads are reasonable and comprise of minimal more than a level in front of the wood and a projection to make prying it off simpler. These spreads can wind up stuck down with propolis on the edges and to outlines, making them hard to expel. Specialists regularly utilize an extending spread that has a band of wood marginally more significant than a hive body, permitting the spread to "telescope" over the crate. An inward spread is utilized with this sort of spread. Bees will at present pastedown the inward spread with propolis. However, it's intended to be effortlessly pried free.

UTILIZING ENTRANCE REDUCERS

Passageway reducers are essential to lessen the size of the first bees need to safeguard. Produced reducers incorporate a little opening and an enormous opening. Start another hive with a little opening, and when that passage gets blocked, you can pivot the reducer to the bigger opening. Numerous beekeepers primarily use bits of scrap wood to achieve a similar goal. Picking establishments and edges for your Langstroth hives can create a lot of dissatisfaction and turmoil for new beekeepers. This convenient guide will enable you to choose what's best for your hives. Pick your establishment type first and afterwards pick your edge type.

The plastic establishment offers the most straightforward and most uncomplicated answer for starting beekeepers since it's economical and more straightforward to deal with than wax establishment. Plastic establishment in wooden casings and plastic establishment in plastic edges give parts that can persevere through the rigours of delivery and the maltreatment of everything except the most unpleasant dealing with. The bees will adjust to plastic establishment only as a wax establishment, and it's frequently brought into brush better and quicker on the off chance that it gets a covering of beeswax. Plastic edges with the plastic establishment are a one-piece plan that requires no gathering, yet breaks in the casing can give concealing spots to bothers, including little hive beetles.

If you choose to utilize a plastic establishment and gather your casings, pick a depression top bar (GTB) and a notch base bar (GBB) for the edge type. After you amass an edge, the plastic establishment primarily flies into the casing. Plastic establishments in wooden casings are as often as possible sold wholly gathered, and the wooden edges take out worries over concealing spots present in one-piece plastic plans that can harbour such vermin as the little hive beetle and wax moths. When purchasing establishments and unassembled outlines, make sure to arrange casings and establishment in their relating sizes. A profound establishment can't fit in a medium edge. Likewise, parts from various makers probably won't be right, so it's ideal for arranging from one producer. Casings for rambles (green) and edges for labourers (yellow)

Beeswax Foundations and Frames

Beekeepers have utilized unadulterated beeswax establishments introduced in wooden edges for over 100 years. Even though it's a conventional decision, the wax establishment has a couple of downsides: It's delicate; it can break in chilly climate and hang in blistering climate, and it will endure under any misusing. A beeswax establishment frequently has its arrangement of confounding casing types. However, the best decision for learners is wired wax with snares. Vertical wires go through the wax, offering help, and they stretch out over the wax and are twisted to shape a snare. The snare fits under the wedge on the top bar and supports the establishment, keeping it from descending. Moreover, including even cross wires will help forestall dropping in the hive and establishment breakdown in extractors.

Amassed outlines with wax establishments either have outlined with a wedge top bar (WTB) and a split base bar (SBB) or edges with a wedge top bar (WTB) and a notch base bar (GBB). The wedge at the highest point of an edge is expelled, the establishment is introduced, and the wedge is then stapled or nailed set up over the establishment to make sure about it. An SBB takes into consideration an establishment that runs profound or droops marginally in the warmth to hang through the bar. End bars ought to have gaps to take into consideration hanging even cross wires.

A GBB requires an exact fit and one that a few providers can't ensure.

Foundationless and Wire Frames

Foundation less casings offer an option for those needing a second choice, wanting a special brush, or inconveniences of introducing a wax establishment. A few producers offer an edge where the top bar has a V-formed wedge. On the other hand, numerous bee-keepers make their own by introducing the wedge from a WTB sideways or sticking a Popsicle stick or something comparably formed in the top bar for a guide. Regardless, the wedge fills in as a beginning stage for bees to assemble establishment in the edge. A foundation less casing introduced between outlines of the drawn brush is usually drawn straight by the bees, however, on the off chance that this isn't possible, a beekeeper should be careful in guaranteeing it's drawn straight by the bees. You may need to me-diate to guarantee it stays straight. Since the bees do not have an establishment for a labourer measured brood, foundation less edges may wind up being for the most part drawn out as automa-ton brood.

Drawing in Swarms to Your Hives

Welcoming multitudes to relocate to your hives is an energizing chance, yet its requests are essential to progress. Realizing where to put your lure hives, how enormous to make them, and what scents pull in honeybees will incredibly expand your capacity to tempt swarms normally.

A setup state is anyplace the bees have chosen to make a home. They'll have begun building brush, and they'll, for the most part, safeguard their home and honey stores. However, a multi-tude is regularly conveyed for province multiplication needs; the bees are engorged with honey despite everything searching for a home, and they're USUALLY very meek. Numerous rushed property holders misidentify set up settlements by calling them swarms. A multitude can discover a passageway into space in a divider or then again tree and become a setup state in days. Multitudes can be as little as softballs or as large as inflatable balls in size. What's more, much the same as with states, not all multitudes will act or appear to be identical.

Utilizing Swarm or Bait Hives

Regenerative amassing begins in late-winter and keeps going through late-spring, and this is the most probable time a multitude could move into your empty hive. Your goal is to make your hive an alluring spot for those bees. A multitude of traps or snare hives should be dim inside, water-tight, and of a suitable size. Utilize an old 8-outline Langstroth box and fill it with old brood brush, and you can purchase a circle you can put over the passage to close it when you're prepared to bring the temporary hive down. Utilizing such a snare doesn't ensure you'll get bees to move to your hive, yet the more you set up in various areas, the almost certain you are to get a multitude or two.

Utilizing Swarm Lures

You can purchase economically produced swarm draws, even though lemongrass oil appears to function too if worse. A couple of drops on a paper towel collapsed inside a sandwich sack left in part open inside a trap hive achieves a moderate arrival of the first oil fragrance that should keep going for half a month. Old brood brush is additionally a decent bait. However, it attracts wax moths. Scouring the inside dividers with beeswax or utilizing old hive boxes puts the aroma of a hive inside the snare and makes for good attractants.

Precautionary measures to Take

Multitudes are a charming method to get freebees, including securing astounding nearby hereditary qualities. Be that as it may, in regions where Africanized honeybees are a worry, you ought to painstakingly screen the new hive for cautious practices as it gets set up and develops. Additionally, because multitude sovereigns are often from the past season and the bees may slaughter her to supplant her, ensure the new state constructs new sovereign cells, the settlement develops. All the bees appear to modify their new home. Robust scents from new paint, synthetic compounds, or sealants may hinder bees. Endeavours to substitute lemon oil or other essential oils for lemongrass oil have indeed been fruitless. Putting honey inside the lure hive will pull in bees, yet these are looters taking the nourishment to their home as opposed to scouts searching for another home.

Multitudes don't get bunch typically in a particular shape. However, they're unquestionably noticeable when they structure! Numerous beekeepers accept that non-domesticated multitudes speak to unrivalled survivor hereditary qualities from bees that have been unmanaged and untreated for quite a long time. In any case, those multitudes may originate from vigorously treated hives around the bend.

Getting Swarms

One incredible approach to find out about bees and beekeeping is to get your multitude. This isn't a perfect strategy for every single starting beekeeper, yet on the off chance that you feel good catching bees, this is a superb prologue to beekeeping. Dealing with Different Swarm Locations multitudes can happen anyplace, and when they do, is set up with the correct hardware and the correct arrangement will assist everybody's with consoling level from yours to the bees'. For most circumstances, these instruments should help:

1) Protective rigging

2) Hive smoker

3) Eight-foot stepladder

4) Cardboard or core (nuc) box

5) Lightly hued bedsheet

6) Bee brush

7) Pruning shears

8) Queen cut

9) Frames

10) Drawn brood brush (if accessible)

Ensure you have a sovereign before going anyplace with your crate of bees. On the off chance that a sovereign is in the container, the bees will probably remain at an opening with their tails noticeable all around, and they'll fan her pheromone to draw in hive mates. Some multitude circumstances incorporate ground-level tree limbs; tree limbs available by stepping stool; such human-made structures as a post box, divider, or fence; and on the ground, which may show harmed or dead sovereigns.

Instructions to CATCH A SWARM

1.   Put on your defensive rigging, place a bedsheet beneath the multitude, and put a container on the sheet and under the multitude.

2.   Use your smoker to help quiet the bees down. On the off chance that the multitude will fit in the crate, go through your stepping stool to move to where the bees are and give the branch a couple of quick shakes. This should cause the vast majority of the bees to fall into the container. Leave the case on the bedsheet and near the cluster to pull in the rest of the bees. (You can likewise knead them with a bee brush onto a bit of old brood brush and afterwards place the brood brush in your multitude box.)

3.   Once you have whatever number bees as would be prudent in the crate, put the cover on the container, leaving enough room toward one side for the bees to travel every which way. In case you're utilizing a nuc box, put everything except one end bar into the case, giving the bees a dull cavity.

Shipping and Installing a Swarm

If the bees will stay in the container for an all-encompassing period (longer than 60 minutes) and the day is generally warm, different jab gaps in the crate to give ventilation. When the catch box is fixed shut, ensure the bees are as agreeable as you are in your vehicle and afterwards take them home to introduce them in a hive. On the off chance that they're in a cardboard/transitory box, you'll have to move them into a hive around the same time or the next morning. You'll require a progressively lasting home accessible for the bees. Freebees without outlines are inclined to overheat. You can likewise discover the sovereign and put her in a clasp or utilize an excluder over the passage for a few days. Queen-less multitudes aren't excessively phenomenal, and the capacity to decide whether a multitude has a sovereign will incredibly improve your chances of effectively introducing it into another hive. When the bees have been introduced, feed them a 1:1 sugar-to-water blend to assist them with chilling off and give them nourishment until they're arranged to their new home.

Sovereign clasp

These bees have relocated to a surrendered owl box—and made it their home. Monitor the crate for a couple of moments to see whether the bees will remain. On the off chance that the sovereign is in the case, the strays will advance to the crate once they understand their sovereign has deserted them. On the off chance that she's still on a branch, expect to see the bees in the crate advance back to the branches.

Allow the bees to experience the entire method; however, utilize your bee brush to knead them onto a bit of brood brush. When you have the same number of bees as you can get into the crate, close it up to get ready for transport. Utilizing brood brush will likewise assist you with isolating the solid bees from the harmed bees.

Different Techniques

On the off chance that you ascend a stepping stool to get to a multitude, take a crate to get them into a holder all the more rapidly. In case you're expelling bees from anything that is not a tree, utilize a bee brush to drive bees into the case delicately. You can purchase and introduce honeybees into their new hive in three usual manners: purchase a bundle of bees with a mated sovereign; purchase a core (nuc) state of bees with their mated sovereign, or then again purchase a full-size state of bees previously introduced in their hive box. Bundles of bees, which commonly weigh around 2 to 3 pounds, are commonly sold by more significant sovereign reproducing tasks what's more, by a business or transitory beekeepers. A bigger bundle is best and holds roughly 10,000 to 12,000 bees, for the most part, working drones, a couple of automatons, and, obviously, a mated sovereign (who's kept separate until you acquaint her with different bees).

The hour of the day when you introduce bees doesn't make a difference. However, bees love daylight and fly, utilizing the sun and light to manage them. They don't usually fly in obscurity, and they don't care to be upset after dull. Favourable circumstances

1) Can be introduced into a hive box

2) Have no wax brushes that could convey remaining pesticides, maladies, or bee bothers

3) Will be bloodless for a few days in the wake of introducing, which will diminish parasite checks and take into consideration progressively successful vermin treatment

4) Have frequently been given an anti-toxin in their syrup to take out nosema and lose bowels

5) Give new beekeepers the chance to watch their bees construct wax and start also laying, developing from the earliest starting point

6) Can be delivered to you (climate and zoning allowing)

7) Docile nature because bundled bees have little to lose and nothing to ensure

Inconveniences

1) Unknown whether sovereigns have been assessed for acceptable creation and laying designs

2) Queens not nearby or accustomed to your locale, which

could mean further costs on the off chance that you requeen later in the year

3)   Delayed province development because the sovereign has little space to lay, bees vanish quicker than they're being conceived, and new states dry for around a month and a half

4)   Needing to take care of sugar water until the hive is built up or there's acceptable nectar stream outside

Have your hive box all set and set up in the domain you plan to leave it before your wrap shows up. Promise it's level, and expel tall grass or weeds from around your hive stand. Precisely when the bees are amassed around the syrup can in like manner, the sovereign, they're set up to introduce. Have a large fixed compartment with a 1:1 sugar-to-water degree blend to manage the bees moving during the establishment. On the off chance that it's pouring, blustery, colder than 60°F, more bubbling than 95°F, or extraordinarily lessen, the bees might be desolate about being moved. If you ultimately should introduce the bees in the dreadful environment, give a valiant effort to ensure about the bees also, rapidly get them into their new hive box so they can start to package again and keep their new sovereign warm.

See how the bees show in the gathering

If they're strolling near or if your sovereign is dead, contact your bee vendor as quick as time awards to ask for a substitution sovereign. You'll notwithstanding everything need to introduce the pack in the hive and present the dead sovereign similarly as she were alive.

Keeping her with the settlement will assist them with remaining dynamically settled considering the way that they can notwithstanding smell her pheromones fanning their wings inside the screen like they're attempting to escape from the container, they may be dry, overheated, or trying to chill off. Given this is legitimate, set them in a cool, lessen spot for a piece before trying to introduce them. You can get in like way spritz the outside of the gathering compartment with a light muddling of plain water or sugar water. Measure what number of dead bees are at the base of the gathering. Routinely, 1 to 2 inches deep could be standard vanish of progressively arranged bees, in any case at any rate 3 inches may mean an issue with your bees or they may have been hurt during transport or breaking point.

Introducing Package Bees

Before starting your presentation, read through all the guidelines. It's marvellous to have a companion help you and even inspect the best approach to you as you travel through the procedure. Start by lighting your smoker (on the off chance that you have to smoke your bees) and wearing your watched pieces of clothing.

1 REDUCE THE HIVE ENTRANCE BY USING AN ENTRANCE REDUCER: a dab of cut wood, grass, plugs, or a sovereign excluder circle. A little state can considerably more suitably ensure a little method for 1 to 2 inches.

2 HOLD THE QUEEN BOX WHILE watchfully expelling the compartment of syrup from the pack, and recognize a dash of cardboard over the opening to shield the bees from flying out.

3 BRUSH BEES OFF THE OUTSIDE OF THE QUEEN BOX, and carefully look at your sovereign for wounds and to ensure she's alive and moving extraordinarily. Watch that any escort bees inside the sovereign isolate territory are besides alive. On the off chance that any have passed on, ensure their bodies aren't hindering the sovereign keep exit.

4 REMOVE THE CORK FROM THE END OF THE QUEEN CAGE that in like way has white treats preventing the gap. Leave shut the end with a connection and no sweets. On the off chance that your sovereign pen has no treats, by then leave the two plugs in and return three days to expel the fitting yourself, lay the dilemma down inside the hive, and let the sovereign exit. Hanging the pen like this will shield any dead escort bees from destroying the exit for the sovereign.

When to Smoke Bee

If you surprisingly crunch a bee during the establishment procedure, it discharges a ready pheromone that gets different bees empowered and progressively inclined to start attempting to sting you. You can smoke that locale to cover the pheromone aromas and shield different bees from taking an intrigue.

1   HANG THE QUEEN CAGE—with the pastries end up—between two edges in the new hive. Assurance the bees approach the screen on the sovereign isolate zone so they can deal with the sovereign and help spread her pheromones all through the hive.

2   REMOVE FOUR OUTSIDE FRAMES FROM THE HIVE BOX, and a brief timeframe later set the gathering inside. Void the cardboard over the opening to permit the bees to slither out. The bees will gather around the sovereign and start examining their new home. Set the spread back on the hive.

3   COME BACK THE NEXT DAY TO REOPEN THE HIVE, pull out the unfilled pack, attentively supplant the four lodgings, and a brief timeframe later close the spread once more. Check for the sovereign assertion in 2 to 3 days at whatever point required or hold as long as multi-week before checking, keeping as a funda-

mental concern that immaterial upsetting effect is great.

Precisely when you check the hive once more, the sovereign ought to be out of her sovereign breaking point and living with the state. You can also glance through the lodgings to see where the bees have added their wax to examine for eggs and new hatchlings. The bees should attract wax on 2 to 3 brushes before the culmination of the significant week. Keep managing the settlement a 1:1 sugar-to-water blend for 4 to about a month and a half. If your bees start to store the sugar water in all the open cells, the sovereign won't have space to lay eggs, which proposes your settlement won't start to make. Despite the way that they may drink the sugar water in a couple of hours or a couple of days, hold up 3 to 4 days before giving them another quart. An inside (nuc) hive is 4 to 5 edges of pulled in brush with bees different stages—from egg to grown-up and it regularly has a youthful mated laying sovereign. Since explicit affiliations sell nucs made out of bees from various settlements, talk about any starting stage questions or worries with your seller before leaving the apiary with any bees.

1) Established state withdrawn brush

2) Laying and acknowledged sovereign

3) Brood all things considered

4) Knowing the sovereign's laying design before leaving the apiary

5) Typically some honey and some dust in the nuc brushes

Disservices

1) Late-season accessibility implies the bees may battle to

endure winter

2) The comb can contain maladies, leftover pesticides, or bee bugs

3) Can grow out of their compartment and be inclined to crowd

4) Unlikely to reap honey during the primary year

When you have your hive prepared, a 1:1 proportion of sugar-to-water blend arranged, your defensive dress on, and your smoker lit, you would then be able to introduce a nuc that as of now has the sovereign discharged to the settlement. On the off chance that the sovereign hasn't been discharged at this point, she'll be in a sovereign enclosure and will require a 2-to 3-day early on period first.

1 REDUCE THE HIVE ENTRANCE down to 1 to 2 crawls by utilizing a little bit of wood, grass, stops, or a sovereign excluder.

2 REMOVE 4 TO 5 FRAMES from the new hive box before opening the nuc, and smoke the nuc—first fresh and afterwards open the top and gently smoke the highest point of the casings of the brush.

Purchasing a built-up hive implies you can hop directly into beekeeping with insignificant beginning exertion. A built-up hive ordinarily contains 7 to 10 casings of brood, typically related bees that as of now function admirably together, and their sovereign. It will likewise likely have gathered assets put away in a portion of the brushes, for example, dust, nectar, honey, and propolis.

1) Can be bought whenever because you're changing the hive's area

2) Possibly having the option to collect honey during the primary year

3) Less time spent thinking about a fully-developed settlement

4) Knowing the sovereign's laying design before purchasing

5) Potential for casings of wax to be defiled with pesticide deposits, bee bugs, or illnesses

6) Stressful for a built-up province to move to another area

7) Larger settlements with more assets to ensure, which can bring about increasingly cautious bees that are inclined to sting when they're upset

1 CAREFULLY PLACE THE NUC FRAMES with bees into space in the hive box. Be mindful so as not to crunch bees or the sovereign. In case you're utilizing a casing feeder on one edge of the hive, ensure the brood outlines with bees are close to one casing ceaselessly from the casing feeder.

2 CLOSE THE HIVE, however, leave the void close by if there are still many bees in it. In the long run, those bees will fly out and locate their new home.

3 IN ABOUT A WEEK, you can check for eggs and hatchlings. If you don't have any eggs or hatchlings inside about fourteen days, your sovereign probably won't have endured the move. Contact an accomplished beekeeper for an assessment or contact your bee vender to get some information about a substitution sovereign.

Introducing a Queen Bee

There are numerous purposes behind introducing a sovereign. Sovereign kick the bucket, on the off chance that you have to supplant an old sovereign or something different has happened that you have a queenless hive, you'll need to rapidly introduce another sovereign to guarantee the hive keeps on having a sovereign bee that will assume control over egg creation.

1 PICK UP THE QUEEN BOX to deliberately look at your sovereign for wounds and to ensure she's alive and moving well. A few sovereigns will have specialist bees inside the sovereign enclosure with them.

2   REMOVE THE CORK from the finish of the sovereign confine that likewise has white sweets hindering the opening. The end without treats and only a stopper in it ought to stay shut.

3   IF YOU'RE INSTALLING THE QUEEN into a hive with drawn brush or establishment, you can press the sovereign box into the brush or lash the sovereign pen to the casing. Be sure you're not blocking bee access to the screen or hindering the exit for the sovereign once the candy is bitten through.

Testing Acceptance

To test sovereign acknowledgement while she's still in the sovereign confine, watch the bees that are covering her enclosure for indications of hostility, for example, twisting their stomach areas around to attempt to sting the sovereign through her pen. You can likewise utilize a gloved finger to dismiss the bees the sovereign confine gently. On the off chance that the bees adhere to it like Velcro, they presumably aren't happy to allow her to live. Hold up until the bees can be gotten over effectively from the confine, showing indications of better acknowledgement. If you locate a dead sovereign in a hive or a sovereign enclosure, leave it inside the hive with the state until you have a substitution sovereign.

Hang the enclosure on a level plane with the screen up or vertically with the candy up. Along these lines, when the bees eat through the sweets, the sovereign can leave the pen, and her exit won't be hindered by a specialist bee that may have passed on and is obstructing the exit.

CHAPTER 3

Maintaining your Hives

Since you've dived in and have your first settlement of bees, you have to see how best to think about your bees and how to perceive when they need a petition or when you should disregard them. In any event, knowing some fundamental science and the whys behind their practices will assist you with settling on choices to their most significant advantage. In this section, you'll figure out how to perceive what the bees are gathering and putting away in the brush and how they utilize those assets. You'll likewise figure out how to settle on the executives' decisions that help them when required. This part is the passage to keeping your state stable and sound.

Life structures of a Healthy Hive

You and your bees can receive more benefits when you realize that your bees have all they have to keep their province energetic. Tips introduced here will assist you with searching for the correct signs of a healthy hive.

Great Brood Pattern

Brood is the term beekeepers use for bees that are still in egg, hatchling, or pupa stages. At the point when your sovereign is stable and creating a decent brood design, at that point you'll realize the hive will keep on flourishing. Search for the accompanying signs of sound brood brush in your hives:

1) Brood brushes that are firmly gathered and close to the focal point of the container on the off chance that they're in a Langstroth hive

2) Cells not skipped—which means the eggs are comparable in age—which makes it simpler for working drones to take care of the brood and keep them warm

3) Almost every cell filled on the two sides of an edge, which is viewed as the best quality level for sovereign efficiency

You ought to have a particular explanation behind opening a hive. Whenever you open a hive for any sort of review, you're disturbing the province and the sovereign, which can put unnecessary weight on your bees and cause long haul hurt. You may need to do some testing to know whether your bees have enough honey put away. If you have a Langstroth hive, you ought to have one box loaded up with honey, which is generally a medium honey super you've added to the hive. This will guarantee your bees have enough honey to endure the coldest part of winter. Furthermore, if not, you'll have to take care of them additional nourishment in fall to permit them to develop more stores before winter, when it's too cold even to consider opening a hive.

Sufficient Pollen Stores

Dust is protein for developing bees, and it's how they get every one of their nutrients and minerals. Bees will generally store the vast majority of their dust in the brood boxes. Generally, each casing will have some dust on it to take care of to the creating hatchlings on each brush. At the point when the bees have heaps of dust or additional dust, they'll put everything into one brush off to the side of a brood region. If you have a littler province that doesn't appear to be developing rapidly, verify whether they need more dust. You can take care of them back their dust on the off chance that you gather it during long dust days and freeze it until you need if you see bees bring forth arbitrarily all through the brush, at that point you may have a sovereign that is maturing or was ineffectively mated. Numerous outer powers climate, temperature, regular changes, inappropriately arranged brood search for laying, the sovereign not being taken care of enough imperial jam, or deficient in general nourishment stores—can likewise add to imperfect brood creation. Consider all prospects before choosing to supplant your sovereign. Or then again, you can purchase dust substitutes at online bee stores and feed it to them dry or in dust patties, which are blended utilizing honey or sugar water.

Propolis

Scavenging bees gather tree and plant sap and take it back to the hive as propolis. They'll utilize this "stick" to cover within the hive just as to fill in breaks or cleft to forestall light, air, downpour, and bugs from entering the hive. Some honeybee species make, what's more, utilize over the top propolis and appear to stick down everything in the hive, making it hard to perform hive investigations. By and large, propolis is an ideal hive item since it's antibacterial and advantageous to the bees, helping keep their home safe from diseases.

Taking care of Bees Safely

Ideally, one reason you've chosen to keep bees is that you like them and need to support them. While bees aren't pets, you should attempt to regard them as others consciously as could reasonably be expected and find a way to protect yourself as well.

A few beekeepers express the best time to open the hive is in the day while the more significant part of the foragers is away from the hive. That works incredibly as long as the climate is coordinating. A spot where it's blistering nearly all year and in case you're wearing a sharp suit, you may think that it's better to assess in the early mornings. Keep water close by, which you can drink through your bee cloak. It's a smart thought to tell your bees you're coming into their region—regardless of whether for a review or another essential explanation. Utilizing a smoker will make your bees begin savouring honey case they have to slip off because they figure they may catch fire. Utilizing a smoker will likewise veil their caution signals, which means the more cautious bees won't assault you.

Abstain from CRUSHING BEES

Whenever you have to move a casing or utilize a hive instrument, do it with care. On the off chance that you haul a casing out too rapidly, you may roll a bee or, more terrible yet, roll the sovereign in the middle of edges or between the divider and a casing, causing injury or passing. At the point when you remove outlines from a container, maintain track of their control and direction so you can return them to their unique situations in the hive. At the point when you return casings to the hive, do so gradually to forestall crunching bees underneath. The ideal approach to stay away from interruptions is to keep them from happening in any case. It's more secure not to bring your pets into the bee yard with you, and if your bees start to pursue one of your pets and sting them, you're probably going to get stressed and occupied, making you drop an edge or leave a hive open to care for your pet.

Since being stung can turn into an interruption, ensure you wear defensive rigging, so you don't drop an edge of bees or want to surge with your errands. Bees distinguish fast developments as a risk and are bound to get unsettled on the off chance that you move excessively quick. Keep your telephone in your home or on quiet.

Bees will assault your most dependent territories first—your eyes, nose, mouth, ears, face, head, and hands-on the off chance that they believe they're under danger. In case you're stung on a hand, expel your rings quickly on the off chance that you get limited expanding. Bees appear to turn out to be increasingly disturbed in stormy and breezy climate. You can utilize a great deal of smoke to free the top from the hive, close the hive and move to an obscure region, get into your vehicle, or move inside to let the settlement quiet down. Although you can't truly be harmed through your bee suit, it's still no amusing to have vexed bees attempting to sting you and conceivably passing on if their stingers are getting trapped in your suit.

Brisk Tips

The ideal approach to forestall an issue is to be readied:

1) Wear security to forestall and maintain a strategic distance from stings.
2)   Have a sufficiently bright smoker and additional fuel to prop it up.
3) Minimize interruptions.
4) Move gradually and purposely while around the hive.
5) Keep a hive open just as long as essential.
6)   Know your cutoff points, and work with an accomplice in case you don't know of your cutoff points.
7) Avoid getting excessively blistering, tired, or got dried out, particularly in sweltering climate.
8) Have a break plan if something turns out badly.
9) Have drug close by in case you're sensitive to venom.
10) Know where your telephone is and ensure you can without much of a stretch access it if you have to call somebody in a crisis.

Examining Your Hives

You may need to keep an eye on your bees for heap reasons, including ensuring they're sound, deciding any issues with the sovereign, and confirming that nothing keeps your bees from approaching their regular undertakings. Before you open your hive, you have to set up the bees for this gentle interruption.

LIGHTING A SMOKER

Smoking your hive permits you to all the more effectively beware of your bees and their conduct, particularly because smoke upsets bee resistance components. Lighting a smoker—and keeping it going while being used—is a crucial initial phase in smoking your hive.

A run of the mill youngster botch isn't placing enough fuel in your smoker to get past the main hive. The other issue with not placing enough fuel in is that the smoke won't be cold enough for the bees. As the fire develops, it can blow hot coals into the air as you puff the howls, and you never need to blow ashes into a hive when you investigate because they can hurt the bees.

1 INSERT A SMALL PIECE OF NEWSPAPER INTO THE SMOKER AND LIGHT IT. Siphon the cries a couple of times to help light the fire. When the smoker is sufficiently bright, add limited quantities of fuel to keep up the fire. Continue siphoning the roars as you go to guarantee the smoker continues smoking and has a little fire.

2 PACK THE SMOKER WITH STICKS, MULCH, OR BARK. When the smoker is consuming admirably, begin pressing it full utilizing higher bits of sticks, mulch, or pieces of cedar bark, puffing the howls once in a while as you go. Utilize your hive apparatus for pressing the fuel and wear gloves to secure your hands.

You won't have to mist the whole bee yard in thick smoke during a hive investigation. Let the predominant wind float the smoke onto the beehives. At the point when you get to the hive, crush the cries, pointing a couple of long puffs at the hive entrance from around 2 feet away. This underlying stream of smoke confounds the gatekeeper bees and ought to send the majority of the bees hanging out at the passage once again into the hive. Let the disarray settle in, and the smell of smoke start to cover their correspondence pheromones before contacting the hive. Honeybees are touchy to vibration, and when you contact the hive, they'll know it—even before you take the external spread off.

Following a couple of moments, pull up the extending cover and send a light puff into the highest point of the hive. Pull off the inward spread and afterwards give another puff after you expel this layer. Give a long puff along the edge as you air out each layer. This sends the bees down into the edges and off the tops. Proceed with this "puff, expel, puff" process as you work your way down into the hive. Each time you break two layers separated, puff, evacuate the top layer, put it in a safe spot, and afterwards puff once more. Give keeping your smoker a shot the upwind side and afterwards expel the casings from the downwind side (as long as that is not a similar side as the passage). This encourages by permitting smoke to delicately keep on floating over the bees, keeping them quiet and your aroma covered by the smoke blowing at you. The objective is to utilize just limited quantities of smoke. If you expertly pack a smoker, it ought to have enough fuel to last the whole visit to most bee yards. On the off chance that your smoker is by all accounts going out, snatch a portion of that additional fuel you carried with you and pack your smoker once more.

You can invert the procedure when you're done with the examination by smoking the bees daintily to crowd them once again into each container and away from the edges, so they don't get crushed as you restack the crates.

Keeping up a Queenright Colony

Nothing is more significant for a hive than a reliable and beneficial sovereign. She's essential to such an extent that each time you investigate a hive, you should discover the sovereign first—or possibly discover signs that a sovereign was there as of late.

Indications of a Queenless Colony

Sovereign during assessments, it doesn't mean she's not there. Yet, you can check for signs that the hive has a sovereign that is playing out her fundamental undertakings. As you acquire understanding as a beekeeper, you'll begin to see that a queen-right settlement has an amicable buzz to it—an even and lovely murmur. Queen less hives, however, are noisier, and the bees will appear to be less sorted out and regularly flee from you during reviews, remembering running off the looks over to cover up for the hive dividers or baseboard.

Physical Signs of a Queen less Hive

On the off chance that your bees are running everywhere inside the hive, that makes it harder to attempt to discover the sovereign. Try not to accept that she's dead or has left the hive. Search for these physical signs that the province is queen less before considering requeening:

1) No new brood: Inspect the hive for recently laid eggs or on the other hand youthful hatchlings. Choose a brood outline, put the sun behind you, and hold the casing up 8 to 12 inches from your face. Edge it to get the daylight to reflect into the cells, and search for minor eggs or C-molded hatchlings in the base of the cells. No eggs or hatchlings likely methods

you have a queen less state.

2)   Too MUCH honey: If you locate that a hive has gotten substantial with honey in pretty much every edge, something is
most likely out of order. Any eggs or hatchlings either, this
implies without a laying sovereign, the bees become foragers and keep gathering and putting away nectar despite no
hatchlings to take care of. You should in any case attempt
to discover the sovereign, and on the off chance that you do
discover her, you have to decide why she's not laying.

3)   Laying laborer's: If you recently had sovereign laying eggs
yet whenever you do an investigation you discover numerous eggs laid in cells or dispersed automaton cells, this feas-
ible methods your sovereign is absent, and a working drone
has begun to lay unfertilized eggs in what will end up being a
bombed endeavor to spare the queen less province.

Restoring a Colony to Queenright Status

When you're sure you can't discover the sovereign or any indications of new brood—and not topped or creating brood—you have
a couple of decisions for requeening:

1)   Order another mated QUEEN. This relies upon a raiser's
capacity to have sovereigns available to be purchased.

2)   Combine the province with a certainly QUEENRIGHT state.
The season and the climate will direct how attainable this
is.

3)   Give the bees an edge of eggs and hatchlings to permit them

to make their QUEEN. You must have a stable hive that can stand to lose an edge of future bees.

Sovereigns are likewise acceptable at stowing away, however regardless of whether you can't discover her and regardless of whether you don't see signs that a sovereign was as of late in a specific hive, don't do anything immediately. Recheck the hive in another 3 to 7 days searching for newly laid eggs or new hatchlings. On the off chance that there are no indications of a sovereign, at that point, you should requeen the hive.

SUPPLANTING THE QUEEN (REQUEENING)

Each hive's endurance relies upon a stable and productive sovercign. Performing ordinary reviews of your settlement to guarantee your sovereign has abundant space to keep laying eggs and that your province has satisfactory sustenance to take care of the sovereign and the brood is basic. A satisfactory brood example of eggs, hatchlings, and topped brood on your casings or can't perceive any brood whatsoever, you may need to supplant your sovereign. You can do this as others consciously as could reasonably be expected, yet it's central to slaughter a sovereign that is not, at this point ready to satisfy her motivation.

1 BUY A NEW QUEEN before doing anything with the old sovereign. Buy this new sovereign from a confided in reproducer, and examine her to guarantee she looks sound.

2 LOCATE THE OLD QUEEN, expel her from the hive box, and slaughter her. You can squeeze her, or you can drop her into a container of scouring liquor to safeguard her to make some sovereign pheromone attractant for a future lure hive.

3 FEED THE QUEENLESS COLONY a 1:1 sugar-to-water blend. This will help the province all the more promptly acknowledge another sovereign since this nourishment reproduces nectar stream. Hold up 24 hours before you present the new sovereign. It's never wonderful to need to slaughter a sovereign. However, a more established sovereign that is coming up short doesn't re-

coup. Your bees can just flourish if they have a stable sovereign that keeps on laying eggs.

4 AFTER 24 HOURS, expel the plug that is over a similar gap as the white sugar treats or marshmallow end of the sovereign's pen. Try not to jab or evacuate the treats, and don't just legitimately discharge the sovereign.

5 HANG OR PLACE the new sovereign's enclosure close to the top and in the middle of two of the brood outlines. Ensure the bees can get to the screen around the sovereign to take care of her and become more acquainted with her.

6 CLOSE UP THE HIVE, and return to beware of her in 4 to 7 days. The bees ought to have eaten the candy to discharge the sovereign, and you should see her strolling around the casings. Check for brood week by week for the following couple a long time to check she's started laying.

A few beekeepers supplant their sovereigns naturally every 1, 2, or 3 years. I like to survey my sovereigns consistently and supplant them varying. I additionally accept that the most advantageous time to supplant a sovereign is in the pre-winter. Another pre-winter sovereign will start laying heaps of new eggs, and you'll have another gathering of more young bees who'll overwinter with the hive. At the point when the hive doesn't crowd, they get more significant and more grounded, which takes into account a colossal number of foragers that are all set during the enormous spring nectar stream. Another sovereign in harvest time implies a bigger brood in the spring—which implies progressively honey!

BALLING THE QUEEN BEE

At the point when working drones need to slaughter another creepy-crawly, they utilize a method called balling. They encompass the other bug with a tightwad of working drones—frequently twisting their mid-region around to likewise sting—that will warm up the centre of the ball to a hot enough temperature to murder the creepy crawly in the centre. They can and will likewise utilize this strategy to slaughter an outside sovereign bee under the right condition. For instance, if you expel a sovereign from a province and give the bees another sovereign before they've lost the old sovereign's pheromone, they may slaughter the new sovereign, which is the reason most new sovereigns are presented gradually utilizing a sovereign enclosure to shield the new sovereign from being balled.

Sovereign Piping

Sovereigns have a piercing sound called funnelling they make to speak with their state and with rival sovereigns. It's kind of a redundant sharp buzz, and you may hear it while acquainting another sovereign with a province and she's been let out of her confine. You may likewise hear it when a province is pursuing a sovereign it doesn't need, or the bees are balling her. At the point when a province has a few sovereigns bring forth at once, the central sovereign to be discharged will frequently pipe and different sovereigns will pipe consequently, accordingly uncovering their area to the principal sovereign, who will go to their topped cells and sting them before they can be discharged, in this manner executing her adversaries for the royal position.

The multitude of Causes and Controls

Amassing is one way a state duplicates. Be that as it may, for bee-keepers, losing more than 50% of a stable province to amassing is frustrating. Figuring out how to perceive and forestall issues that can trigger amassing is an administration aptitude you'll need to ace. Albeit expanding its number of labourers and gathering and putting away heaps of honey are useful for a settlement, the bees will crowd on the off chance that they become packed or need more space for multiplication. Your bees will frequently emit cautioning signs first:

1)   Brood home refilled with honey and brood creation cut back rashly

2) Swarm cells—frequently on the base or edges of the brush— being loaded up with regal jam and hatchlings Not any more additional searches for putting away honey, making the bees start refilling the brood home Honey or dust stopping up the brood home, and the sovereign has no space to lay more eggs

Adding supers to give the bees more space for putting away honey Expelling brushes of honey and adding void edges to permit the bees to draw wax, the sovereign to lay eggs, and the bees more space Conceptive Swarming to bunch the bees have likely been moving in the direction of this objective since the past winter by going into that winter with abundant stores of honey to assist them with building their numbers up rapidly in the late-winter. That gives them the ideal opportunity to amass enough stores after they split to endure the following winter. A more seasoned sovereign absconds with the province and abandons a developing new sovereign that should be Insufficient fruitful space for all the bees to bunch close to the brood home and the sovereign, prompting swarming A lot in and out traffic clogging the brood home Adding a super to the hive to give your bees additional bunch space Adding top access to give foragers an approach to travel every which way without going through the brood home to store honey in her resulting marital mating trips to assume control over the state.

Making an Artificial Swarm

At times, it's simpler to part a hive yourself before the bees swarm all alone than to ceaselessly attempt to make more space for them in a current hive. With only a couple of activities and two or three apparatuses, you can partition a hive by empowering a counterfeit multitude. To make a counterfeit multitude, take the old sovereign and everything except one edge of open brood with all the medical attendant bees and move them to another container in another area. Try not to let any sovereign cells make it into the new hive or, in all likelihood when they bring forth; they'll execute the old sovereign if she doesn't crowd. This new hive won't swarm since it won't have foragers or sovereign cells. Leave the old hive with all the topped brood, one casing of eggs and open brood, no sovereign, and some empty supers. This should shield the old hive from amassing because they are queen less and don't have a lot of open brood. You can leave a couple of sovereign cells in this hive in case you're not giving them another sovereign. If you are giving another mated sovereign to them, you should demolish all the sovereign cells and check again in around five days that they haven't made more. This strategy works best in the spring—directly before the principle honey stream.

Since sovereigns bring forth 15 to 16 days after the egg was laid, if you see sovereign cells, you just have likely 6 to 8 days left before the multitude takes off. Nearly when the sovereign cells are topped, the settlement will get ready to take the old sovereign off to the new area they've been exploring. Keep some sovereign cells in an old hive in case you're not presenting another sovereign.

Controlling Overcrowding

Congestion in hives happens when assets and ventilation are lacking. This regularly happens during spring, when brood creation can make a hive extend too rapidly, and it can compel your bees to crowd—all of which you'll need to stay away from by making precaution strides. Giving your bees a case of establishment for a Langstroth hive will give them more space to extend the settlement varying. They probably won't perceive undrawn establishment as accessible for use if the brood home edges have topped honey above them or if a sovereign excluder has been put underneath the undrawn establishment. Bees are frequently reluctant to go through a sovereign excluder to work undrawn establishment situated above them. During extension, a province can become dust or honey-bound if an edge of durable dust or topped honey is excessively near the brood outlines with no void attracted brush between. Likewise, the sovereign wouldn't, in general, like to traverse to the opposite side of

Opening the Sides of the Brood Nest

Opening the external edges of a brood home can give your bees the required space to venture into a mass of dust to lay more eggs at the tops and sides. Contingent upon the season and the size of a state, you can include another edge in an external situation in the hive and bees with adequate nourishment will draw new establishment and give the sovereign space to lay eggs. It can get distressing for the bees if you move the brood around inside the hive. It's smarter to assemble two brood casings to permit the bees to be additional productively watch out for them. Numerous bee-keepers split single hives into equal parts or split out a little state in the spring to debilitate the benefactor hive, to forestall amassing, and to make another settlement to compensate for any winter misfortunes. When the multitude encourages has introduced itself—with sovereign cells at the base or then again sides of an edge—the best choice is to move the sovereign and a portion of the bees to another crate in another area. With the sovereign proceeded to stuff eased, the now queenless settlement ought to acknowledge a recently brought forth sovereign and wait.

Making a Simulated Swarm

A genuine re-enacted swarm includes shaking the sovereign and a large portion of the bees onto new edges (however don't shake outlines with sovereign cells), making more seasoned bees fly back to the first hive. With no brood to raise (or on the other hand only a single casing), these young bees—with hardly any required assets—will draw brush rapidly also, can make excellent brush honey if a stable nectar stream exists.

Putting away and Using Drawn Comb

Honeybees consume a ton of vitality building wax for putting away honey; however, if you take a couple of steps to ensure their drawn brush, you can give it back to them during the next honey stream and twofold honey creation. Drawing brush is when bees assemble their wax cells on the establishment you give them in the casings. Having extra boxes of the drawn brush can incredibly expand a honey reap. However, nothing is more unsettling than having your put away brush destroyed by bugs. When the honey has been collected, little hive beetles have little intrigue. However, wax moths can rapidly plague the brush, with dull brood brush being appealing to moths. Treat extricated brush with paradichlorobenzene (PDB). Stack the removed dry supers around five high and spot 6 ounces of moth precious stones on a paper plate or a square of paper in the top super.

Ensure all breaks are taped closed; you're essentially making a fumigation chamber. Check your stacked supers each 3 to about a month and a half if you live in a warm atmosphere because the moths may get once again into the stacked supers and lay more eggs when the PDB has disintegrated. Let some circulation into the search for a few days before returning them to a hive. Try not to utilize mothballs; they have synthetic concoctions that will enter the wax and are dangerous for bees and people. You have to introduce another sovereign, or if something—or something —has harmed or on the other hand annihilated a few brushes inside a hive. You can supplant harmed brush with put away drawn brush.

Recordkeeping

Keeping precise records permits you to follow medicines, climate conditions, sovereign issues, bother issues, and another hive movement. This encourages you to recognize what functioned admirably and what didn't, particularly on the off chance that you add hives to your apiary.

Settlement Records

If you have numerous hives, you could number them, paint every one an alternate shading, or name them to assist you with keeping track of everyone. Also, in case you're in your bee suit, you may think that its most effortless to convey a marker with you to compose notes on the hives, which you can decipher and substance out with subtleties later. Some data you may note include:

How you keep a record is an individual inclination. A few choices remember composing for a hive, making a database spreadsheet,

1) The date of the review furthermore, who performed it
2) The assignment utilized for a specific hive
3) Equipment parts and their conditions
4) The state of the hive
5) The sovereign's hereditary qualities (whenever known) and her establishment date
6) The hive's demeanour
7) Whether you see the sovereign or any sovereign cells
8) Whether you found any eggs, automatons, or irritations
9) The hive's populace

Different APIARIES

You may choose to keep your bees in various bee yards. You could have one scratchpad for your home apiary and another note pad for your out yards. Ensure your assignment framework is something you record—on the off chance that you're not generally the one doing the assessments. Attempt to assess at any rate (however close to) 10 hives one after another. You'll need to allow yourself to determine any issues as opposed to attempt to investigate every one of your hives in a single day.

What develops in your general vicinity at some random season will help not just illuminate you about the condition your bees live in. However, it will likewise assist you with supplanting or evacuate any plants if issues emerge. As you stroll around your apiary or bee yard, you can record the date and what's in sprout. Notice which plants your bees visit, as this can help foresee bee conduct and rummage conditions. It additionally causes you to realize when you may need to take care of your bees sugar syrup or dust in light of deficiency conditions. It's likewise enjoyable to recognize what your bees are gathering from when you reap their honey. Since specific preferences and scents are unpretentious, having a blossom journal will enable you to realize what mixes of plants made your honey.

DIFFERENT CONSIDERATIONS

1)   Legal DOCUMENTATION: Make sure to keep buy or tenant agreements, hardware manuals, and even any enrollments you have for your apiary or your beekeeping business together with other beekeeping records. You ought to likewise ensure your hives and hardware are stamped or marked with a name that effectively distinguishes it as your property.

2)   Expenses and duties: If you're keeping bees as domesticated animals for a farming property charge assessment, following beekeeping-related pay and costs are required by your neighborhood burdening authority. Check the assessment code for your particular region to get some information about the number of hives required per section of land, extra documentation required, and the recording cutoff time. You'll additionally need to follow mileage, salary, and costs identified with selling honey or other beekeeping things.

You ought to perform standard keeps an eye on your hives, your bees, and the general condition. Albeit numerous undertakings are the equivalent regardless of which hive type you have, bee action (or deficiency in that department) will regularly direct when and how you investigate your hives.

WHAT ARE YOU LOOKING FOR?

Generally tally what number of orderlies she has in her entourage just as what number of bees face her, encompass her, feed her, and focus on her. The more bees that take care of her needs, the more advantageous she is—and the more grounded her pheromones are to draw in them, spreading a feeling of prosperity all through the province. If you see eggs or youthful hatchlings, you presumably have a sovereign—or if nothing else you had a sovereign as of late. Review a casing to check whether the sovereign's laying design is predictable all through, and tally what number of cells are loaded up with brood, including what number of are working drones and what number of rambles. Likewise, check for sovereign cups or sovereign cells.

Ensure that brood outlines are secured with bees, which means most of the open brood has grown-up bees in the region for taking care of and keeping the temperature kept up. You may see different bees out on the edges of the brood home structure new wax on new brushes. New wax is a lot lighter in shading, it's excellent, and it smells like honey. As the bees use it and trample it, it gets darker from year to year. On the off chance that the bees are overlooking you during an examination, that is a decent sign. On the off chance that they're flying around when you get an edge, on the off chance that they're attempting to escape from you, or if they're knocking your cover or attempting to sting your gloves, they're unsettled. Here and there, it's smarter to wrap up rapidly and close the hive to let them quiet down.

Plentiful Nutrition and Food Storage

The bees, for the most part, have put away dust and nectar on the edges of the brood outlines. Ordinarily, bees store honey over the brood; this is known as a honey crown. They store dust on the sides or along the base of brood casings to take care of the hatchlings. What number of various shades of dust would you be able to see? An assortment usually implies the bees are getting a balanced eating regimen. Imperial Flight a completely mated sovereign once in a while flies on account of the heaviness of her mid-region loaded with eggs, however, if she flies, she'll rapidly land furthermore, for the most part, attempt to come back to the wellbeing of her hive.

Working drones are taking care of the hatchlings in a couple of uncapped cells. You should additionally research them and afterwards attempt to determine them:

1) 	If you see gatecrashers anyplace close or in your hives —from ants, little hive beetles, or wax moths or hatchlings to cockroaches, wasps, arachnids, or varroa vermin, you'll need to decide how best to kill them.

2) 	Discoloured or darker hatchlings, depressed gaps, or clingy or gooey cells or honey could be indications of sickness or parasites.

3) 	Deformed or wilted wings on the bees, spread wings on more slow, ungainly moving bees, as well as vast quantities of dead bees, pupae, or bee parts on the hive floor are additionally a reason for concern.

4) 	Chewed wax cappings on the hive floor could mean burglarizing has happened.

5) Track how overwhelming each hive feels when you lift them exclusively. Additionally, do the edges feel overwhelming with honey and dust or do they feel light and void?

6) Listen for sounds from your hives before you open them. Contrast them and how the hive sounds once you open them. What you hear may tell you about an interloper or a queenless hive. Likewise, if the sounds change starting with one edge then onto the next inside a similar hive, you can more readily disengage any issues, even though bees will regularly cause stronger commotions as you to draw nearer to their sovereign.

7) If your sovereign is channelling—emanating a loud commotion that seems like a peep—this could mean potential clash. Virgin sovereigns will funnel to different alarm sovereigns and working drones that they're willing to battle for sovereign status.

8) If you smell rot or an unpleasant scent, check for indications of sickness or form on the brushes. Heaps of dead bees on a baseload up can in some cases smell awful, yet, typical hive smells are light and sweet. A thick sweet smell could mean little hive beetles are getting into the honey.

Examining Your Hives

Make the strides in the "Lighting a Smoker" segment before following these general rules.

LANGSTROTH HIVES

1)   Take safety measures to forestall squashing or harming your bees when utilizing any instrument to open your hives.

2)   Make sure the sovereign isn't on a hive spread when you expel it from a hive.

3)   Remove outlines gradually from a hive to forestall any wounds to any bees strolling around the brush.

4)   Start assessments at all populated zones of the hive to abstain from pounding or rolling a sovereign.

5)   Remove the second casing in from a side divider before expelling the first outline. Since the bee space between the divider and the first edge may be abbreviated, evacuating the second edge first will forestall wounds to the sovereign or any of the bees.

6)   Inspect each side of each casing as you expel it to guarantee the sovereign isn't on that outline. If she is, place that edge close to the first hive body on the off chance that she chooses to bounce off the casing. She'll fall once more into the crate without injury.

7)   Stack your edges to permit you to return them to the hive in a similar request. Ensure the stacked edges additionally face a similar course.

8)   After you return the edges to the hive, find the sovereign to guarantee she hasn't taken off. Examine her to ensure she hasn't been harmed.

9) Once all the edges have been come back to the hive, push them to the focal point of the hive, leaving additional room at the external edges to limit burr brush working between outlines. You can likewise utilize an edge spacer apparatus to equally circulate the edges once they're all back in the crate.

10) Before you return the spread to the hive, try to blow two or three puffs of smoke over the crate to get the bees to descend into the casings and away from the stacking edges where they are bound to be crunched.

In focal Texas, because our harvest time stream has a lot of goldenrod blossoms when I open the hive, it can smell similar to dirty rec centre socks! Not every single terrible stench are an issue.

THE BEEKEEPER'S TIPS

Since I have a lot of hives and outwards, when I go to review, I'm usually taking a gander at 8 to 10 hives in succession. I put a bit of channel tape on the posterior of each hive body, and I utilize a marker to record a couple of shorthand notes following every examination. I can compose progressively particular notes when I return to each hive to peruse my notes.

This will assist you with seeing the eggs and little hatchlings in the bottoms a lot simpler. Since a top bar is a horizontal hive, the bees start toward one side and gradually work toward the opposite end. For an examination, you need to smoke the hive entrance and under the spread and afterwards expel a couple of top bars from the end the bees aren't yet utilizing. After you pull out one to two bars to begin, puff some smoke in to tell the bees you're coming in. This additionally allows them to alter, and on the off chance that they're not in the temperament, they'll start leaving the hive by the hundreds, and you can rapidly close the hive, but the bars and the top back on, and leave.

Proceed with the assessment by pulling out around 8 to 10 empty bars and put them in a safe spot. Gradually unstick and move over any of the different bars that don't have anything put away on them yet. When you get to the bees, slow down and start seeing them bar by bar, putting each bar successively withdraw before you—yet to the vacant side away from the passageway you're moving in the direction of.

CONTRAST FROM LANGSTROTH HIVES

The most significant contrast with top bars is that you can't tip the bar sideways to investigate the cells. When a bar has wax, bees, honey, dust, and so forth., in it, that casing will be excessively substantial and too delicate to even think about tipping side to side. You need to keep the bar on its pivot, turning it around end over end, so the brush is either hanging down, confronting sideways, or hanging topsy turvy. Wax brush is delicate and will snap or sever when it's warm, cold, or substantial. Indeed, even the best-built hardware can inevitably have issues that require fix or substitution. A couple of upkeep steps can help delay to what extent your hive boxes last–and how solid and glad your bees will be. Water sprinkling from the beginning boxes or gathering inside a hive on a baseboard can speed up wood decay. One approach to limit or forestall harm is decent paintwork— one layer of preliminary and two layers of a decent outside paint offer brilliant assurance from the climate.

Try not to utilize paint on inside surfaces, and abstain from painting the top and base edges where hardware surfaces meet. Paint in those spots will make the crates hard to get separated later. On the off chance that your hive has free paint, scratch it off and sand the hive before applying new paint. The first line of protection is decent paintwork. Free paint should be scratched and sanded off, and splits in outside creases or joints ought to be caulked. You can fix outside hive harm with wood clay, and you can fix splits in outside creases and joints with caulk, yet don't utilize clay or caulk inside your hive. If the corner joints in a container have loosened up and consider development, put the waterproof paste into the holes, drill pilot openings, and use screws to fortify those corners.

Most gear sold as "collected and painted" would profit significantly from more paint before beginning use. On the off chance that the base of your hive has termite harm or wax moth harm—which you can tell from the football-formed divots eaten out of the casings and inward dividers—you can rescue your hive by cutting off 1 to 3 crawls from the case. This implies a profound box would turn into a medium box, and a medium box would turn into a shallow box. Decay in the base of your hive brought about by an organism that can, in the long run, obliterate the auxiliary uprightness of your hive—you can slice 1 to 3 crawls of harmed wood from the container. Wood decay in top and base sheets, it's ideal for supplanting the harmed hive box because there's very little you can rescue.

UTILIZING PROPOLIS AS A PROTECTANT

Bees will generally utilize propolis and wax to cover and ensure within their case. Propolis and wax, for the most part, ensure the upper edge and edge rest of a container. Edge rest fix is certifiably not a reasonable alternative since wood clay presents cruel synthetic concoctions, and metal wraps set casings higher than planned and present concealing spaces for little hive beetles. Casings are fundamental for hive soundness. Having great attracted brush your casings is a beekeeper's fantasy, and you'll need to ensure those brushes. You can fix broken top bars on wooden edges (and even plastic casings) by utilizing an edge saver to help strengthen outline corners. It's regularly simpler to supplant broken base bars. An edge cleaning device makes cleaning wax from the furrows in wood outlines speed up. (Not utilizing one barely appears to merit cleaning the wax.) You would then be able to fix cross wires and introduce a new establishment.

You ought to turn out the more established darker brood brushes following a 5-year most fabulous utilization time. Since brush ingests and holds any potential synthetic compounds or contaminants that the bees may have followed into the hive, following five years, they may have developed to levels that are poisonous to the bees. A simple method to turn brush out is to pull out two casings for each time of the darkest brood brush from each crate and scratch all the look over out to dissolve down for beeswax. In a 10-outline box, evacuating two casings for each year will put you on a 5-year turn plan. You won't have any desire to evacuate them at the same time since it takes a great deal of bee vitality to make the wax brushes in any case, and the bees reuse them to spare time and honey. The drawn brush is a valuable asset. Furthermore, you can help offset the vitality consumption with state wellbeing and prosperity through ordinary brush revolution.

Someone of a kind favourable circumstances to top-bar hives makes it the favoured style for some start (and prepared) bee-keepers: no crates to lift or stack, no extractor to purchase, and a full-length perception window. Despite these advantages, top-bar hives despite everything expect to learn and adapt, be that as it may, these tips and deceives should help. You can diminish the odds of a slip away from a top-bar hive, particularly in case you're starting with a multitude or a bundle. At the point when you start with a nuc, the bees have brush and brood to deal with; however, with a bundle, the bees need the motivation to remain.

1)   Beeswax: Make it smell like home by utilizing beeswax to rub or dissolve and dribble onto the edge of the top bars. Or then again far superior, hang a piece or two of old brood brush if you can get some from another beekeeper.

2)   QUEEN EXCLUDER: Use a sovereign excluder over the passageway to shield the sovereign from flying out until she begins laying eggs. Along these lines, the working drones will discover this is home and that they have a sovereign to satisfy—and keep sound.

3)   Feeding: Always feed another bundle or a multitude in the hive itself, so the bees don't need to go rummage for nectar to start wax building. Make the nourishment simple to get to so they barely need to work at all and can get going structure new look over for the sovereign to lay eggs in.

I've placed another multitude in a top-bar hive with a sovereign excluder and observed all the bees fly out and swarm up to a close-by branch to trust that their sovereign will go along with them, but since she can't, they'll return to the hive to discover her. They may leave once more, and however, inevitably they appear to make sense of that the sovereign is home to remain, and they return into the hive and get the opportunity to work making it their new home.

TOP-BAR HIVE CONSIDERATIONS

Top-bar hives don't typically utilize edges or establishment, albeit some have been altered for that. You can believe that the bees realize how to fabricate their brush, with the goal that isn't the issue. Yet, in an original hive, the looks over are never pulled out for an examination and can in this way be propped and cross-supported to follow furthermore, balance out them inside the hive cavity. At the point when you perform examinations, take care to secure their brush as you move it around. New white brush is the most delicate and will twist effectively on the off chance that you tip the brush sideways. They were worked to hang with gravity, so remember gravity when you control them to save their shape. Another tip for those beekeepers in areas with climate boundaries—hot and cold: Empty wax brushes that get extremely cold can snap off the bar on the off chance that they're knocking. At the point when temperatures move to higher than 90°F, limit hive investigations, yet on the off chance that you do open a hive, attempt to keep brushes out of direct daylight and get done quickly or less so the wax doesn't dissolve.

Placing bees into a top-bar hive void of brush implies the bees get the chance to choose where to start connecting all the new brush, and the decisions they make aren't always helpful for beekeeper examinations and the executives. You'll need to make some continuous and standard examinations to get the bees building where and how you need them to assemble. Now and again, they'll expand on more than each bar in turn or manufacture their brush connection focuses in a curve shape, which is more grounded for holding the heaviness of honey or bees, however that can make reviews troublesome or chaotic, best case scenario. When the bees have made one decent straight brush, you can utilize that search as a guide for future brush working by putting a vacant bar in the middle of the divider and the first brush. The bees at that point have a straight guide on the two sides to make bee space between, and they will construct another straight brush. You can keep setting an unfilled brush in the middle of two straight brushes until there are roughly 10 to 12 bars filled. At that point, there's sufficient straight brush to control the hive and keep it on target.

On the off chance that they're assembling another brush askew, you can pull the brush and simply tear the abnormal segment and push it onto the bar where you need it, and the bees will fix the tear and reattach the brush. Top-bar hives, for the most part, improve in tropical and subtropical atmospheres instead of in areas with times of long virus winters. A favourable position of a Langstroth hive is that vulnerable climate if the honey super is stacked over the highest point of brood group, the glow from the bees usually rises upward into the honey chamber. It makes it simpler for the bees to eat while remaining warm. In a top bar, all development is horizontal, and on the off chance that it gets incredibly chilly, the bees can't move a long way from the glow of the group, so they can freeze or starve once they've eaten all the nourishment inside closeness to the warm bunch.

Before harvest time shows up, ensure the brushes with honey are near the brood home, and put some on either side, sifting through any vacant brushes to be put more distant from the brooding territory or evacuated out and out. Having honey on the two sides of the brood region likewise gives them additional protection. In a 4-foot top bar, it assists with utilizing an adherent board—or a divider board—to isolate the top bar into littler functional space for the state. As the bees develop, you can move the divider board more remote, giving them progressively more space. At either edge of the brood, territory to permit them to sporadically include more brood look over for the sovereign to lay eggs in. This permits them the moderate development they have to develop without giving them a lot at once to ensure. It's the inverse in the winter when the state starts contracting. It may be essential to pull a portion of the additional brushes if the bees aren't covering them. You can securely store them and give them back again throughout the spring development season. You can likewise contract the accessible space in the hive that the bees need to keep warm by moving the adherent board back nearer toward the brood bunch. This will likewise permit them to spare their vitality.

UTILIZE SOLID BOTTOMS FOR BETTER MANAGED HIVES

Likewise with any hive, the discussion over secure or screened bottoms proceeds—and top-bar hives are no particular case. One favourable position of a screened base is in case you're utilizing powdered sugar to battle varroa vermin; the overabundance powder can drop through the screen. Then again, full screens permit an excessive amount of wind stream in a top-bar hive, which in the winter can be hazardously cold for the bees and they in this manner make some hard memories keeping their brood group sufficiently warm. You may likewise observe a decrease in brood raising at the bottoms of the brushes; the bees don't will in general put brood inside the base couple creeps of a screened base.

Albeit many top-bar hives have a base screen with a removable spread, when hive trash falls through the screen onto the spread beneath, on the off chance that the bees can't get beneath the screen to tidy up the trash, at that point, it makes a putrefying rubbish heap that can turn into a concealing spot for such nuisances as little hive beetle hatchlings, parasites, and wax moths. Top-bar hives have bunches of various structures, yet there ought to consistently be an approach to decrease the passageway to keep out any undesirable bugs and particularly bees from different hives. The passage ought to be limited for winter or when ransacking happens and toward the start for another hive or a littler province to give it less space to safeguard. You can utilize stopper gaps toward one side of the hive to limit the number of open doors. In the late spring, you may utilize every one of the four doorways, leaving the main one open to take into consideration heat escape. In the winter, the top passage is always plugged closed to help hold in the collected warmth. In case you're doing an assessment and notice a great deal of debris and jetsam at the nonworking end of a top-bar hive, at that point you can unplug that gap to allow the bees to clear it out rapidly without moving the trash right down to the passageway end past all the brood and bees. Think about it an alternate way. However, it could likewise fill in as free passage for a more significant state or be utilized for additional ventilation when required.

CHAPTER 4

The Bee Harvests

Probably the best thing about the connection between a beekeeper and your bees is the prizes of collect time. Pretty much everything a honeybee produces has esteem to the beekeeper: honey, beeswax, dust, and substantially more. You'll locate no preferred satisfaction over tasting that first honey reap from your bees a flavour that is exceptional to your particular territory. In this part, you'll find out about how to utilize items from the hive as elements for other fun items, including candles and healthy skin fundamentals. You'll likewise learn different approaches to utilize items from your hives all made by bees you've made the most of their business.

Results of the Hive

Numerous individuals think honey is the main result of a hive. However, a hive produces many astounding items that have captivating and flexible employments. Honeybees transform their gathered assets into items people need to eat, gather, and use. It's an incredible association in case you're mindful to leave enough for the state's needs when you collect these items.

Honey

We consider beekeeping is that we keep bees to get honey. Honey tastes superb, and beekeepers overall are glad for their neighbourhood honey regardless of whether it's only for individual use or on the off chance that they decide to sell it. In the United States, the USDA has three honey evaluations (A, B, and C) given ascertaining scores for different rating factors:

1) MOISTURE content: level of water
2) Absence of deformities: the absence of particles, propolis, and dregs
3) Flavour and fragrance: taste and smell from the principle flower source
4) Clarity: straightforwardness and absence of air bubbles

Honey likewise has shading assignments that don't influence the review; however, determine the honey's flavour with light honey being gentle and darker honey being more grounded:

1) Water white
2) Extra white
3) White
4) Extra light golden
5) Light golden
6) Amber
7) Dark golden

All honey usually contain peroxide action, which is a piece of the explanation honey is antibacterial and doesn't ruin as long as it's kept dry and in a fixed compartment. Honey is likewise hygroscopic, which implies it can without much of a stretch retain dampness from the air around it, making it considerably increasingly significant for you to get dampness far from it.

Beeswax

Even though bees use beeswax to store honey in cells and to secure developing hatchlings and pupae, you can utilize beeswax for making a few unique items, including candles and healthy skin items, just as being an added substance for nourishments. Regal jam is delivered in the hypopharyngeal organ of medical attendant bees and took care of two youthful hatchlings and to the grown-up sovereign bee. The bees don't store illustrious jam; it's continuously taken care of new. During sovereign raising, nurture bees flexibly an excess of it to sovereign hatchlings, and what goes uneaten will aggregate at the base of the cell. Since the sovereign has supersized ovaries and lives any longer than working drones, there was a lot of hypothesis during the 1950s that maybe if individuals somehow managed to eat imperial jam that they would be increasingly ripe, look more youthful, and live more—however, these were rarely demonstrated.

Propolis

Propolis or bee stick is created by honeybees who gather sap and other natural pitches from trees or plants and blend it in with spit and beeswax. It's utilized to seal splits and holes in the hive. You can gather propolis from a hive by scratching it off edges or hive dividers, or you can utilize a plastic propolis screen trap inside the hive. Numerous narrative reports depict the different medical advantages of utilizing propolis, for example, assisting with colds, sore throats, wounds, pimples, ulcers, consumes, and some more. One organization even makes a toothpaste utilizing propolis to feed and secure gums. Dust is stacked with protein, nutrients, and minerals. Numerous individuals can verify that ingesting limited quantities of nearby dust every day causes them to fabricate personal invulnerability to occasional sensitivities. Some dust sustenance considers you have likewise demonstrated an expansion in red and white platelets, decreased cholesterol, what's more, brought down triglycerides.

Bee Bread

Bee bread is protein-rich nourishment and can be eaten by people. It's an essential resource for settlement wellbeing and winter endurance. Searching bees gather dust and take it back to the hive. They empty the dust straightforwardly into open cells close to the brood and close to honey stores, making a band of dust, which are commonly known as bee bread. Numerous new beekeepers find that cutting brush is an incredible way, to begin with, their new side interest. It's not as chaotic or as tedious as separating honey or wax, and cut brush offers numerous healthful advantages when eaten. In case you need to sell items, you get from your hives, beginning with a cut brush is perfect. If you cut Dust brush honey, you should freeze your search for in any event 48 hours. This murders the eggs and keeps them from incubating inside the bundling.

This additionally murders wax moth eggs in the drawn brush; however, it doesn't keep moths from getting to the brush and laying eggs once more. If your more relaxed space is satisfactory, you can store the cut brush in there. You'll have constrained achievement on the off chance that you have a go at fixing the brush in plastic packs and putting away it outside your cooler. Province and you care for bees and can part them into another hive, at that point you can sell the subsequent hive or keep it and use it to deliver progressively honey and different items. Bringing in cash by selling bees by parting a hive or selling a sovereign in bundles, nukes, or on the other hand full-size hives is challenging to work a productive Endeavor however for a beekeeper with a growing apiary.

Setting Up Your Honey Extraction Space

Honey extraction is something your entire family can appreciate. With just a couple of provisions, you can bottle your raw honey for yourself or impart to loved ones. Own honey extraction space. This tote will get all the wax tops from the honeycombs on the edges. Since honey extraction can turn into a muddled procedure, purchase a tote that is 6 inches down, 3 to 4 feet in length, and 18 to 20 inches wide and accompanies a top. The perfect space is encased, warm, which assists honey with streaming more straightforward—and has a lot of space for gear.

Extractor

Various sorts of extractors exist. Littler extractors commonly have hand wrenches, while ones that hold at least six edges are frequently electric. A few extractors have plastic tanks, yet bigger tanks are treated steel to forestall rust. They utilize radiating power to toss the honey from the uncapped cells onto the dividers of the extractor. The honey at that point sinks to the base, and a valve permits the honey to stream into a tote or can. Nourishment Grade Storage Containers is a plastic can with a top. However, it should be made with nourishment grade plastic. You can ordinarily get them in 1-gallon, 2-gallon, and 5-gallon sizes from a nearby home improvement shop or buy a used one from a neighbourhood bread kitchen.

Hot Knife

You can purchase an electric uncapping blade, or you can utilize a blade you as of now have, for example, a serrated bread blade.

If you utilize a bread blade, heat some water, plunge the blade into the water until it's hot, and afterwards cut the wax capping off the honeycomb cells. You can, in any case, cut the capping with a virus blade, yet it's not as simple. Make a point to cut the capping over the uncapping tote, and spare the capping to render them into beeswax. You'll utilize these devices to uncap wax capping's and discharge the honey. An uncapping roller is a gadget with spikes everywhere throughout the moving surface, though the uncapping scratcher has metal tines for penetrating. Which one you use relies upon how little harm you wish to cause to the brush. The screen will get a large portion of the wax particles and any bee parts, so your honey is prepared to bottle and eat. A few beekeepers utilize a bigger measure screen for the first run and afterwards, a minor check miniaturized scale channel before packaging to help forestall honey crystallization. Small particles of wax and dust in the honey can accelerate the procedure of crystallization, yet practically all thick honey will, in the end, take shape.

1)   Hot blade
2)   Uncapping Roller
3)   Hand-wrenched distracting extractor

Step by step instructions to Remove Bees from a Super

A smoke board utilizes a synthetic smell the bees don't care for—discover one that will annoy your bees yet not, in any case, hurt them, for example, Fischer's Bee-Quick—and it pursues them from the honey supers. A smoke board utilizes a synthetic smell the bees don't care for—discover one that will disturb your bees yet not, in any case, hurt them—and it pursues them from the honey supers.

1   MAKE A FRAME a similar size length and width as a honey super however just 3 to 5 inches down. Utilize some felt or material to cover one side.

2   SPRAY THE CHEMICAL onto the material, and set it over the honey supers instead of their top. Inside 5 to 15 minutes, a large portion of the bees will leave the honey supers.

3   PULL THE CAPPED HONEY SUPERS off the hive, and put them into plastic totes with tops or complete them of the bee yard and into a different structure that is secure from bees and creepy crawlies.

Spot the smoke board on the honey too after you splash it. Brush bees tenderly or, more than likely, they won't respond as compassionate to you. You can utilize your bee brush or a lot of long grass to brush the bees off every super and each casing individually. When you have a casing freed from bees, you should move that outline from the bee yard or move it to an encased box to shield bees from the social occasion on it once more.

Utilizing Bee Escapes

Bee escapes are single direction valves you can put between the brood home and the honey supers you're disengaging from. It has a departure the bees can exit through, yet they can't get back up into the super. The most straightforward approach to utilize them is to put a couple of honey supers in a stack on the internal spread with the bee departure and trust that all the bees will exit down into the brood chamber. It can take somewhere in the range of 15 minutes to 3 days for the bees to leave; you'll despite everything have a couple of tenacious bees to get over before gathering.

EXTRICATING AND FILTERING HONEY

When you've expelled the bees from the honey supers and have burglarized their honey, you'll need to remove that honey from the topped casings. This can turn into a muddled procedure, however, once you taste that new crude honey, you'll realize it was all justified, despite all the trouble. There are two sorts of edge extractors: distracting and outspread. The majority of the littler hand-turned extractors are unrelated, which implies the flat side of the honey casing faces the mass of the extractor, and they can remove just the outside substance of the honey edge. You'll have to flip the casing to disengage the opposite side. Purchase plastic or treated steel extractors since they won't rust. You'll likewise need to purchase nourishment grade bearing oil to keep the heading dashing. Any extractor you use ought to have a honey entryway valve at the base of the tank.

REMOVING HONEY

1- SLICE OFF THE WAX CAPPINGS. Utilize your serrated blade to cut off the wax capping's into one of the enormous cans. This gives you access to the cells.

2- LOAD THE UNCAPPED FRAMES INTO YOUR EXTRACTOR. Each space with a casing, make a point to equally appropriate and adjust the edges in the extractor. Make a point to have the honey entryway open while turning out honey in such a case that the tank gets excessively profound with honey; the casing spinner will stall out in such honey.

3- Put a nourishment grade can come with a screen or sifter over it under the entryway. During the extraction procedure, the wax will begin to stop up the screen. You can utilize a spoon to evacuate the wax and add it to the wax capping's, which you can gradually strain later.

UTILIZING EXTRACTED HONEY

TURN THE CRANK ON YOUR EXTRACTOR.

Start to gradually and step by step get a move on to compel; however, much honey from the cells as could reasonably be expected. The honey will hit the dividers of the extractor and slide down to the base and out the honey entryway, through the sifter, and into the container. Give your honey settle for a few days access the fixed basin. Any wax bits will ascend to the top. Take a sheet of saran wrap and lay it delicately over the highest point of the honey in the can. Cautiously lift the plastic up and off the honey, and it will pull all the wax from the honey, leaving only the raw honey, which is presently prepared for packaging.

One extraordinary advantage to beekeeping is your capacity to gather honey to eat an action you can manage without an excessive amount of work. However, on the off chance that you wish to impart your honey to other people, there are some essential additional means to take. Think about Food Safety, possibly you've heard that honey is the ideal nourishment since it never ruins. That is right—yet it relies on a couple of critical components:

1) You must keep honey in a fixed compartment, so it doesn't ingest any extra dampness. Water will weaken the honey.
2) Every time you open a honey holder, moistness can sneak in. Utilize littler compartments in case you're not going to utilize honey regularly. This will limit stickiness influen-

cing your honey.

3) Honey has a pH somewhere in the range of 3 and 4.5, making it very acidic what's more, microorganisms and life forms can't live long in an acidic domain. This is terrible for those creatures yet extraordinary for you.

4) Bee catalysts separate honey into two side-effects gluconic corrosive and hydrogen peroxide, and we as a whole recognize what hydrogen peroxide does to germs. This is the reason honey has such incredible medical advantages.

Some honey affiliates over filter the honey they bottle and even expel the characteristic dust in the honey, basically deleting its mark. When the particles are evacuated, it's hard to demonstrate where the honey originated from or then again if it's even unadulterated honey. Since a portion of those particulates is dust which has their advantages you ought to limit filtration. Glass containers, canning containers, or those plastic bears are perfect for packaging and putting away honey. Regardless of what you use to store your honey, ensure you purchase a cover that seals and reseals well. Nobody will need to eat honey that has been demolished by outside contaminants before packaging honey, cleans and sanitizes the compartment and the cover. To get the honey into a container or jug, you can utilize something with a pour ramble or a pipe, or you can place the honey into a container or tank with a valve or honey entryway.

Make a point to leave a little air hole between the highest point of the container and the top. You don't need the honey leaning against the top while away. I genuinely like the old square glass Moth bottles that utilization plugs for fixing. Be that as it may, take care to keep the stopper and jug top clean to get a decent seal. In case you're selling your honey, you have to remember some data for a name:

1)   It must have the primary name of the item—honey—and

can likewise incorporate the plant or bloom of the essential botanical source, for example, Orange Blossom Honey.

2)   If the central fixing is honey, at that point, you needn't bother with a fixings list, yet on the off chance that you included different fixings, you should show them in a standard fixing articulation.

3)   You should likewise have your contact data and the name and full location of the maker, packer, or merchant (where the honey is packaged) on the first name.

4)   You must print the net load of the honey (short the jug) in pounds/ounces and metric load on the base third of the name.

Other than these fundamental marking necessities, you should check with your home state where you intend to offer your honey to perceive what different laws you should conform to sell your honey.

Honey Extraction in a Top-Bar Hive

Keeping bees in a top-bar hive implies you won't have to buy an extractor, which is utilized uniquely for extricating from surrounded hives. To loot and concentrate honey from a top-bar hive–and afterwards, appreciate that flavourful nectar.

You can likewise cut the honey off the bar out in the bee yard, drop it into the container, and afterwards set the bar back into the hive and let the bees clean it. This can begin a looting circumstance in your apiary, so use tact. The bees construct brush as they need it (typically brood brushes first) down toward one side of the hive body—and afterwards manufacture honey stockpiling brushes later. You can help deal with the honeycombs by keeping them down toward one side of the living finish of your top-bar hive. I like to have one casing of honey for each casing of brood to overwinter the state, however on the off chance that they store additional honey, you can burglarize it and concentrate it for yourself.

Evacuating the Comb

Before you start, put on your shroud and gloves and light your smoker. As you open the hive, blow puffs over the hive entrance and the top bars.

1 STARTING AT THE UNINHABITED END, pull out 5 to 10 top bars to make some space to work through the hive.

2 COUNT THE BROOD BARS and the fixed honey bars. If you have more honey bars than brood bars, get a new honey bar, dismiss the bees, but the bar into a can or tote, and put the cover on the repository. Rehash this progression for every additional honey bar. You can either take care of the cut brush or put the cut brush into a container and afterwards fill the rest with healthy honey. You can likewise utilize a natural product press to squeeze brushes and gather honey. See "Packaging and Labelling Honey" for how to store honey.

3 ONE AT A TIME put each bar on a perfect cutting load up and utilize your blade to remove probably the best new white brushes to make cut brush honey. Brush on the top bar as a guide for the bees to utilize when they revamp.

4 WITH THE REMAINING COMBS, wear gloves or utilize clean hands to squash the honeycombs over the pail with a sifter appended. When you squash the more significant part of the brush and honey begins to come out, you can hurl the squashed wax into the sifter to let it keep depleting. Let the basin sit for the time being to deplete however much honey as could be expected.

Gathering Wax

While the vast majority need to get honey from hives, you can discover numerous utilizations for beeswax. You have to refine your crude wax to make it increasingly usable. Bees eat roughly 7 pounds of honey to make 1 pound of wax. Beeswax arrives in an assortment of hues from practically white to a dull brilliant green contingent upon how old the brushes are and what they were utilized for in the hive. The wax from the honeycomb is generally the lightest and considered increasingly attractive. Beeswax smells like honey, and beeswax candles consume cleaner and longer than different kinds of candles. Utilize lighter wax capping from honey extraction for your healthy skin items and spare the darker wax from old brood search for candles. To utilize the wax, you gather from your brushes; you have to dissolve and clean the wax. The conventional technique includes a stewing pot, as these guidelines detail.

1 FILL A TEFLON-COATED CROCKPOT most of the way with water and turn the temperature to about 200ºF.

2 PUT IN THE WAX you scratched from the brushes, and let it heat up. The wax will dissolve rapidly and skim on the water.

3 Slow cooker and let it cool. When the wax cools to a strong, you can without much of a stretch get the wax off the water. Notice that energetic particles have settled to the base of the wax.

4 USE A KNIFE TO CUT OFF THE SOLIDS, leaving you with a spotless block of wax.

You can likewise soften the wax without the water, pouring the liquefied wax through a paper towel into a bowl of water or a form. The stable particles will gather in the paper towel, which goes about as a channel. When you have enough cleaned wax, you can remelt it and empty it into flame melds or little wax shape and afterwards sell it by the ounce or on the other hand use it in healthy skin plans to make moisturizer bars and lip ointments.

THE END

Leave a review of my book. For us authors, they are essential for improving and writing other useful content for readers! If you liked "Beekeeping for Beginners" Leave Five Stars!

CLICK HERE

https://www.amazon.com/review/create-review/error? ie=UTF8&channel=glance-detail&asin=B088HGCKPW

Written By Rohn Garden

www.ingramcontent.com/pod-product-compliance
Lightning Source LLC
Chambersburg PA
CBHW070846250726
48662CB00003B/1386